John Reed:
Witness to Revolution

Reed at work in his Greenwich Village apartment in 1916.

John Reed:

Witness to Revolution

by Tamara Hovey

George Sand
BOOKS

Los Angeles, California

Distributed to the trade by Capra Press
P.O. Box 2068, Santa Barbara, CA 93120.

To my nephews
David, Daniel, Robert, and Paul

Acknowledgments

I should like to thank Howard Greenfeld and my editor, Norma Jean Sawicki, for their advice and encouragement in the preparation of this book. I am indebted for research assistance to Carolyn Jakeman of the Houghton Library at Harvard and to Mary Isabel Fry, Virginia Rust and Valerie Franco of the Huntington Library. For their help in obtaining and reproducing photographs, I am grateful to James Ufford of the Photographic Department of the Fogg Art Museum at Harvard University, Hazel Kingsbury, Priscilla England, Tatiana Koudriavtseva and Serge Hovey; to Nina Ratiani I owe special thanks for her generous aid in obtaining photographs from the State Archives of Film and Photodocuments of the Soviet Union. I wish to extend my thanks to Galina Erofeyeva for her assistance in translating Russian documents and to Frieda Lurie who made it possible for me to visit the former Winter Palace,

Smolny Institute, the Kremlin and John Reed's grave. For their personal recollections of John Reed which they so kindly shared with me over the years, I owe an incalculable debt to close friends of Reed's who are no longer living—to Mabel Dodge Luhan, Sonya Levien, Carl Hovey and Mike Gold. To Harry Carlisle, as well, my sincere thanks.

Foreword

Once "John Reed" was nothing more than
the name of an unknown young man out of Portland, Oregon, with a menial job on a New York
newspaper. A short decade later, it was the by-line
of the most widely read American journalist in the
world, whose work has come down to us, more than
half a century later, undiminished in impact. What
was responsible for his remarkable development?
In great measure the qualities of the man himself.
Events did the rest.

When John Reed arrived in New York in 1911
to embark upon a literary career, he found himself
in the midst of a radical political turbulence. Dis-
satisfied to remain a mere spectator, he turned participant, making his own turbulence, adding his
talents and energy to the staggering series of upheavals that marked his era—bloody industrial
strife, a rebellion in Mexico, a world war, a social-

ist revolution—and earning for himself the label "Storm Boy."

His coverage of a strike of silkworkers in Paterson, New Jersey, in a manner then unique not only of digging out a story at its source but living with the people who were making it, gained him an instant reputation as a reporter. A year later, with his on-the-spot newspaper and magazine stories of the Mexican civil war which were gathered into a book, *Insurgent Mexico*, he became the most sought-after and highly paid man in his profession. A few years later still, after covering the Great War on both the western and eastern fronts and after turning out many articles, short stories, and another book, he wrote his classic *Ten Days That Shook the World*, an expertly documented, dramatic account of the Russian Revolution . . . all of which have caused him to be acclaimed as the "father of modern journalism."

John Reed died at the age of thirty-three, and his brief but brilliant passage on earth became a legend over which many people have puzzled. They knew of his work, but what of the man? How was it that a boy born to wealth and privilege had grown up to turn his back on the material comforts he might have enjoyed, to live so intensely the life of the oppressed about whom he wrote that at last he became at one with them both personally and spiritually? How was it that an overprotected child, weak in body and cowardly in heart, had grown into an adult who would ride through bullets and brave imprisonment again and again along his adventurous path? How was it that a boy, whose forebears, for the most part, were hardheaded businessmen and society women of few creative gifts, developed into one of the most dramatic literary talents of his time?

John Reed, in his stormy career, wrote many stories about the paradoxical lives of others. This is the story of his own.

Tamara Hovey
Paris
September 1974

one:

John Reed was known to his schoolmates as a great teller of tall tales. One tale he did not make up though, and which not a soul in Portland, Oregon, at the time could deny, was that he had been born in a castle. Even if they had not seen it with their own eyes, people had heard of the gray mansion, modeled on a French château, which stood on the topmost heights of their city and which was surrounded with a beautiful park and formal gardens. It belonged to John's grandmother, Charlotte Green, and it was called Cedar Hill.

There, on October 20, 1887, Charlotte Green proudly announced the birth of a grandson. In an impressive ceremony at the fashionable Trinity Episcopal Church, the child was christened John Silas Reed. His young parents then took him back up to Cedar Hill where they lived with Mrs. Green and where John spent the first nine years of his life.

The vast estate was an unusual playground for a

1

small boy. There was a glass grape arbor in the garden and tame deer roamed the grounds. There were stables housing the thoroughbred horses that pulled the smart carriages John Reed's late grandfather, Henry Green, had imported from across the seas. There was a lawn terrace below the house where his grandmother would give lavish parties on summer nights. The terrace was framed by fir trees fitted with gas jets which shot flaming lights over the dancing couples.

The château was not only John's first home but in a way it was also his first schoolhouse. There were no formal classes but John, a sensitive child, learned from watching the people around him. Each one taught him a different sort of lesson.

His grandmother, a headstrong woman, was receptive to anything as long as she could find some excitement in it. If her lively and extravagant parties caused the members of Portland's high society to recall their Puritan New England origins and to frown disapprovingly (though they came to them willingly all the same), she didn't mind. She herself belonged to one of the city's wealthiest families and allowed no one to dispute her right to do as she chose. On one occasion she took off for Egypt to ride past the pyramids on the back of a camel and this only added to her reputation as an eccentric. She was more than that, though; she had a discerning eye. Although John was a sickly child, she saw through his frailty to a hidden, untried strength, and after his little brother, Harry, was born she remarked that while Harry was a lamb, John was a lion. Charlotte Green's defiant yearning for new experiences was not lost on John—he himself was possessed by it all his life.

John Reed's father, Charles Jerome Reed—or C.J. as everyone called him—was a New Yorker who had come to Portland to represent a prosperous New York firm and to supervise the sales of its agricultural machinery throughout the Northwest. He was prosperous himself and well liked, especially for his keen wit. His droll stories brightened the dull business luncheons at the exclusive Arlington Club which had elected him its president.

But C. J. Reed was not a light-headed man. He had a serious mind and many secrets. Secrets about his father-in-law, the late Henry Green, who had arrived in Oregon relatively penniless and had become rich by swindling Indian tribes out of precious furs and then using the profits to build water, gas, and iron empires—and the château on Cedar Hill. Secrets about the graft and corruption and even the outright, if "legal," theft that had piled up more than one of the great fortunes of Portland's leading citizens.

These secrets C.J. would lay bare one day when President Theodore Roosevelt appointed him a United States marshal, with the responsibility of exposing the scandalous robbery of public lands by railroad and lumber interests and the network of bribery which ran from petty clerks through federal judges up to the United States Senate. Endangering his career, his social position, even his life, C.J. would become a hotheaded and boisterous crusader for social justice. But, when John Reed was still a child, that day had not yet arrived, and C.J. knew no other way of reconciling those secrets with the pious hypocrisy around him except through his rare sense of humor. If John understood less than half of the amusing quips his father made at the expense of Portland's solemn dignitaries, it was of no consequence—he was getting his first lessons in social satire.

John's mother, Margaret Reed, was more conservative than her own unorthodox mother but, beneath her dainty fastidious ways, there lurked an urge to enjoy the pleasures of life which she took little trouble to hide. Though she was a busy socialite and left John in the care of a nursemaid, she never ignored him—there was always a third eye at the back of her head which watched over her delicate son. As his grandmother did, she, too, encouraged the boy's spirit of exploration and in a way that would influence his whole future—she taught him to read and introduced him to the world of literature.

One of John's closest companions in the big stone house was the Chinese cook, Lee Sing. He was not a servile domestic, but an independent man who owned a shop in Chinatown. From there he would

4

bring John and his brother lichee nuts, Canton ginger, and firecrackers. On many an afternoon at Cedar Hill, John would sit on the high kitchen stool, his spindly legs dangling over the rungs—for he was an undersized boy throughout his childhood—while Lee Sing's agile hands were carefully drying Mrs. Green's Royal Worcester cups or decorating a freshly baked cake for one of Mrs. Reed's tea parties. Lee Sing would tell him about idols and ghosts, about the customs and ceremonies of the Chinese. The impressionable child beheld visions of bloody feuds, of brazen gongs and fluttering red paper, and he became filled with fascination for people of other races and foreign lands.

Often John would be sent to his room to rest, by his nursemaid of the moment, or by his protective mother who was always anxious about his uncertain health. There his imagination would be further stirred by the heroes he found in books. History intrigued him and he plunged into narratives of kings and clashing men-at-arms, into stories of the Arabian nights and of King Arthur's noblemen of the Round Table. But his reading didn't stop there. He found Mark Twain equally enthralling and Blackmore's *Lorna Doone* and, when he ran out of fiction, there was always Webster's Unabridged Dictionary.

During the years John spent at Cedar Hill, he could wander at will over the vast empty estate, but he was not allowed to associate with those his

5

family considered the commoner sort and this, just because it was forbidden perhaps, made him curious about the people who lived down in Portland across the Willamette River. They had no glass grape arbors to wander through, no ponies to ride, but at least there a boy could play as roughly as he chose and do what he wanted without someone telling him that he shouldn't, that he couldn't, because he was "different."

It was that difference that troubled John at times, for it made him feel set apart—an outsider. Of course he had his parents' love, he knew, and he returned it, and he especially admired his father. If the latter never told his son what he wanted of him, the boy nevertheless sensed that, whatever the path he chose when he grew up, he would be expected to be a fighter and a leader. This suited him in a way, for it blended with the heroic visions of the characters he admired in his reading. But at the same time, he had an urge for other things too, for what he didn't have. He wanted to be with ordinary, everyday people and to share their warm and unknown pleasures. He wanted—in fact, he longed for—the other side of the river.

For the moment, there was nothing he could do to reach it, so it is not surprising that during the long days he lived as a shut-in behind the iron grill of his grandmother's estate, he began to write. From his imagination came ideas for romantic and chivalrous stories which he jotted down in a hasty

6

scrawl. Then there were plays he made up and which, when he was a little older, he produced in the attic, with the help of his brother Harry. Finally he composed a comic history of the United States. In a sense this was John Reed's most important work, for it was at the moment of writing it that he made up his mind—as he later recalled in his unfinished autobiography, *Almost Thirty*—to devote his life to becoming "a great poet and novelist."

However, the nine-year-old boy did not feel "great" at all, standing awkward and ill at ease on the noisy playground the first day of school. He tried to cover his discomfort among all those strange boys, who already knew each other, by what he hoped was an insolent stare. At first he was excited about school but a succession of dull and unimaginative teachers merely succeeded in producing in him a tough resistance to all formal learning except in subjects—such as elementary chemistry and English poetry—that struck his undisciplined fancy.

His parents had left Cedar Hill and had moved down into the city, on the "right" side of the river, where John was attending a private school, the Portland Academy. He was closer to that other world he wanted to join, but still the next years were one uphill battle after another against the poor health that kept him out of games others could play and that made him feel, and oftentimes act, like a coward. Some of those battles he won, others he lost.

He lost one to a boy from Goose Hollow, which was a slum district where tough children who later grew up to be prizefighters and baseball players lived. John had to walk through the neighborhood to reach school and the boy threatened to beat him up unless he gave him a nickel. The boy got his nickel.

However, he did win a victory over the others' faint contempt for him with the ingenious stories he made up. They grudgingly began to accept him, because they found he wasn't totally useless. After all, it was he who could tell them who they were— daring Apache scouts or brave Robin Hoods chasing through Sherwood Forest—when they raced through the wooded hills behind Portland during their games. And it was he who could explain to them why they were reclining on couch cushions like ancient Romans, when he invited them to his house for an "imperial repast."

The summer John was ten, his parents took him east to visit his paternal grandparents. Later he remembered the trip in disconnected images—the fierce summer heat, vermin in a boardinghouse where they lived, steam trains roaring on the elevated tracks. That same year he felt a severe pain in his left side and the doctor was called. The diagnosis, kidney trouble; the cure, none. For the next six years he was kept in bed for weeks at a time whenever he suffered an attack.

He fought illness the way he had fought cowardice, in fits and starts, and, as before, sometimes
winning, sometimes losing. He seldom played baseball or football, knowing he couldn't keep up, but
on the banks of the Willamette River, it was the
others who were left behind as they watched him
swim farther and dive from greater heights than
any of them.

As he grew into his teens he began at last to find
his place among his contemporaries—as budding
poet, as class scribe, as editor of the school paper.
During his last year at Portland Academy his kidney attacks suddenly ceased and with this illness
behind him, he felt equal to anyone around him.
He was sixteen now—tall, with greenish brown eyes
and with features which, though oddly mis-
matched, partly sensitive and partly rough, made
him a singularly striking and even handsome young
man. He was burgeoning with unexpected strength
and when his parents decided to send him away for
two years of preparatory school in the East, he felt
more than ready.

But though an upperclassman at the Portland
Academy was a Somebody, a beginner at the Mor-
ristown School in New Jersey was a Nobody, and
Reed had to start all over again as an outsider.
This time he started with less timidity and hesita-
tion. The first day of football practice the boy from
Oregon was out on the field. He ran awkwardly,

threw long and swift passes which went sailing through the air to land out of bounds, was flung to the ground again and again but bobbed up, impatient for the next play. The coach laughed and shook his head—this gawky string bean of a boy didn't have the least bit of skill or polish but his energy was phenomenal; he would make a good player.

With the same energy he plunged into the bull sessions at night in the dormitory. Whatever the subject—politics, religion, sex—he had, at least to his mind, something important and decisive to say. He was always there with a bold remark or a strong argument and always determined to hold the floor with his spectacular tales of the Wild West or the fabulous Green château. Fact or fancy, it didn't matter—he would win his listeners with his gift for storytelling.

In a strict boarding school there is no one more respected than a rebel against authority, and the rigid regulations at Morristown offered John Reed's talents a wide range. Soon ropes were flung out of bedroom windows after "lights out," and whispering boys, with a gangling six-footer at their head, crept down into the darkness to spend the night on the town, only to creep back just before dawn. When country dances were given by nearby schools, John and his classmates would walk in uninvited and calmly steal the surprised girls from their partners. A group of dignified ladies, visiting the Morristown School one day, were appalled to see that someone had placed a chamberpot upon the helmet of a suit of armor. Reed was put on probation after that, but he didn't care—he had gained the admiration of his classmates.

While others could also play football and invent pranks, there was one thing Reed could do better than anyone else around him and that was to write. He began to compose stories and poems for the school magazine. Then he put out twelve issues of a comic paper, the *Rooster*, filled with jokes, some funny, some not so funny—but again that didn't matter. Only one thing mattered; that everyone of the sixty students at Morristown School knew who John Reed was at the end of the first year. He was a Somebody.

But Reed himself was not certain if that somebody he had become was his real self or merely a role he had created. Oftentimes he suspected the latter. When he did, he turned to poetry, feeling beneath his hard-won popularity a strange solitude, a sense of insufficiency. It was at such a moment he wrote the lines:

> *An atom in this world of might and night*
> *I stand alone.*

And, perhaps thinking of himself, he described a violin "singing happily and laughing" ...

> *Then it dies away and leaves us*
> *Something wanting in the night.*

11

When he returned to Portland after his first triumphant year at Morristown (triumphant socially but not academically), he spent the summer thinking about what it was that he felt was missing from his picture of himself as a man. Up until now his romantic idols had been the heroes he had found in books. But suddenly he discovered a real flesh-and-blood hero—and in a most unexpected place—his own home.

C.J. Reed had received his appointment as United States marshal and was pursuing a desperate struggle against corrupt politicians. John saw him dismissed from the presidency of the Arlington Club. He saw C.J.'s former friends swearing he would never again be received in respectable society if he pursued his "ridiculous" investigation. He heard his father being called a "traitor" by rich men whose graft he was exposing, and when a man in the East was shot and C.J.'s own life was threatened, he saw him laugh it off with undiminished humor. John learned more perhaps, sitting in his father's office, than he had from any class at school.

Though he would leave Portland eagerly once again and would return only rarely as an adult, the boyhood struggles he had waged with himself and with others had left their mark. The marks were there for life, ineradicable. And John Reed would always remain, in some deep and inviolate way, a boy from Oregon.

two:

Reed entered Harvard College in September of 1906 along with seven hundred other freshmen. In later years some of them would remember him as the nervy fellow from out West who had ambled irreverently through Mount Auburn Cemetery one Sunday afternoon to leave his card on the tombstones of the most illustrious Boston families with the message, "Sorry you weren't in when we called." Others would remember the time he had been "rusticated"—that is, put under strict professorial surveillance off campus in Concord—after an impulsive spring vacation trip to Bermuda when he had earned his passage back selling poems to a newspaper but had arrived days late for classes. And then, of course, there was the time when he had "sassed" the dean and boasted about it afterwards.

But school grounds had always represented for Reed not only playgrounds where he could indulge

13

to risky limits an irrepressible bent for mocking authority, they were battlegrounds as well. He would never forget his loneliness as an outsider during his first months at the Portland Academy and at Morristown. When he arrived on the Harvard campus, he was determined to fight his way to popularity and distinction there, too. But he did not trouble to assess the obstacles that lay in his path—a rigid caste system and a wealthy student elite that dominated and controlled the exclusive college clubs and all extracurricular activities. He simply plunged, without caution or forethought.

He made no attempt to earn laurels for himself as a scholar, however. Despite the fact that he had barely passed his entrance examinations to college, he no doubt would have been capable of considerable academic achievement, if only he had set his mind to it. In an intelligence test at the Portland Academy, he had scored highest in his class. But along with an ingrained resistance to formal education, Reed had an instinctive feeling that, even at Harvard, the distinction he coveted would be found in other areas. Though he signed up for a routine set of first-year courses—Latin, English literature, French, German, history and philosophy—he eagerly turned his eyes elsewhere.

First, he went out for freshman football, but the competition was severe and he was almost immediately eliminated by the coach. Then he tried to make freshman crew—working at nights, on Saturdays, and even during holidays at a rowing machine in the empty boathouse—and was the last man to be dropped before the squad went to New London. Later he made an effort to become assistant manager of the varsity crew and worked around the clock to earn support for his candidacy. He won the post, but only on paper; the manager, who considered Reed "not quite the right sort" extended the enrollment, and a boy with the more illustrious name of Belmont hurried to New York to get his father's help and that of a name even more illustrious in financial circles, Morgan. Belmont was given the post.

Reed nevertheless hid his disappointment and began to devote his time and energy to the college magazines; if he couldn't win recognition with his biceps, he would at least try to win it with his pen.

He submitted pieces to the Harvard *Lampoon*, a comic journal popular among the undergraduates, and was pleased to see his first submissions accepted. A more serious literary magazine, the Harvard *Monthly*, was a target of even greater prestige upon which the aspiring writer in him soon set his sights. The men on its editorial board were already distinguishing themselves with talents that would lead them to notable careers as professional writers —Hermann Hagedorn, editor in chief during Reed's freshman year, John Hall Wheelock, and Lucien Price. Their example inspired Reed to produce some of the best work he had turned out so far—

15

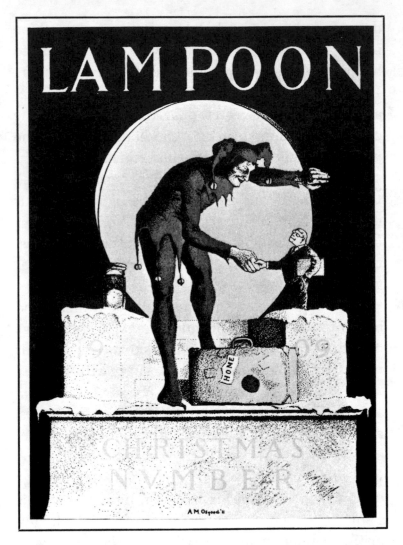

During his Harvard days Reed contributed comic stories to the Lampoon *and served on its editorial board. This cover was designed by Alan Osgood who shared an apartment with Reed a few years later in New York's Greenwich Village.*

the sonnet "Guinevere" and a romantic short story, "Bacchanal." Though at first Reed was but one of the *Monthly*'s contributors, later he served on the board and had a responsible voice in planning and producing the magazine.

But to excel in one closed corner of the world was not enough for him. He had learned as a child to hate niches that confined his spirit. The shadow of the closed iron grill at Cedar Hill would fall across his mind all his life, making him determined to break down any barrier that blocked his way. In addition, though still a fledgling, he had a writer's curiosity to explore all unfamiliar corners of experience, a writer's curiosity to know the people around him whoever they were.

During those early days, however, he simply could not make friends no matter how hard he tried. Often he would follow classmates in the Yard on the way back from lectures and attempt to start up a conversation. While they would answer politely enough, they would never invite him to their rooms, and when he met them again at undergraduate gatherings they often did not even recognize him.

Basically, most Harvard men did not approve of Reed because his western candor and impetuousness were not part of their eastern code of behavior. They came from the most aristocratic families in the country and Reed, they felt, was too open and

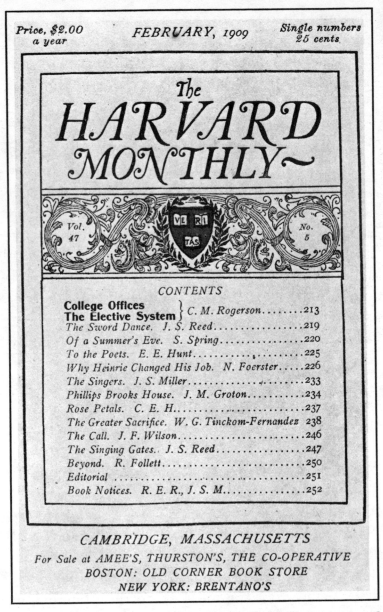

Price, $2.00
a year

FEBRUARY, 1909

Single numbers
25 cents

The
HARVARD
MONTHLY~

Vol. 47

No. 5

CONTENTS

College Offices } C. M. Rogerson........213
The Elective System
The Sword Dance. J. S. Reed.................219
Of a Summer's Eve. S. Spring.................220
To the Poets. E. E. Hunt...................225
Why Heinrie Changed His Job. N. Foerster.....226
The Singers. J. S. Miller....................233
Phillips Brooks House. J. M. Groton...........234
Rose Petals. C. E. H.........................237
The Greater Sacrifice. W. G. Tinckom-Fernandez 238
The Call. J. F. Wilson.......................246
The Singing Gates. J. S. Reed.................247
Beyond. R. Follett...........................250
Editorial 251
Book Notices. R. E. R., J. S. M..............252

CAMBRIDGE, MASSACHUSETTS
For Sale at AMEE'S, THURSTON'S, THE CO-OPERATIVE
BOSTON: OLD CORNER BOOK STORE
NEW YORK: BRENTANO'S

The Harvard Monthly *often featured Reed's poems and* short stories.

The editorial board of the Harvard Monthly. *Standing behind Reed* (seated second from the left) *is his college friend and editorial associate Walter Lippmann.*

exuberant to be the "real thing." Besides, it was clear that he wanted to be liked, and this aroused their contempt. It meant he was pushy. If a man was worth knowing, it was easy enough to find that out; meanwhile, he ought to remain quietly in his place.

Reed rankled under these constant rebuffs and felt a deep misery which he could not communicate to anyone. In his unfinished autobiography, *Almost*

19

Thirty, he wrote: "I didn't know which way to turn, how to meet people. Fellows passed me in the Yard, shouting gaily to one another; I saw parties off to Boston Saturday night, whooping and yelling on the back platform of the street-car, and they passed hilariously singing under my window in the early dawn. Athletes and musicians and writers and statesmen were emerging from the ranks of the class. The freshman clubs were forming. And I was out of it all."

One lonely night when he was standing before a bookstore window, his eyes roving aimlessly over the books on display, he heard someone at his side make a comment. He glanced up in the hope that perhaps here at last was a student ready to form a friendship. But it was merely an elderly professor. They fell into a conversation, however, about the books in the store window. In the course of it, they discovered a mutual liking for O. Henry and the next thing Reed knew the professor had invited him home for dinner. Over their meal they covered every subject from the undergraduate clubs at Harvard to comic opera, talking till far into the night. As Reed at last rose to leave, his host asked his name which Reed told him and then in turn he asked the man his own. It happened to be William James.

William James, one of the most illustrious of American philosophers and psychologists—and a teacher at Harvard. Was Reed really so out of it all? Or was there perhaps another Harvard which had nothing to do with athletes or exclusive clubs?

In the course of his next few years at college, Reed discovered that second Harvard. It was the Harvard of those who had been silently suffering from the same exclusion from campus life that had caused him so much pain. They banded together, in what Reed later described as a "renaissance," to create a means of expressing their own social and intellectual attitudes, a community in which they themselves could act, speak, shine, and be heard.

Their initial move was to form clubs, and how different the meetings were from the narrow gatherings of the Harvard aristocrats. The Cosmopolitan Club, which drew into its membership students from twenty different countries, offered a forum for the exchange of ideas on international events. At one meeting there was a heated debate on executions in Spain. At another, the participants argued about the problem of trade unionism in France. At still another, the topic was the revolution in China. In all of these Reed was an enthusiastic participant, for here were the sort of bull sessions for which he had been thirsting.

Then the Dramatic Club was created. It was inspired by George Pierce Baker's classes in playwriting, which formed over the years such future playwrights as Eugene O'Neill, Sidney Howard, and S. N. Behrman. The club devoted itself to the production of original plays written by graduates

The Cosmopolitan Club to which Reed (front row center) *had been elected president.*

and undergraduates. Reed threw himself into its activities. He became assistant manager, badgering performers into coming to rehearsals, worrying night and day about properties and scenery, running about Back Bay raising money for productions and writing publicity notices for the press. He loved the hard work and the challenge and he also loved the glamour of opening nights.

Later he wrote and staged a play for the Cosmopolitan Club. The piece was inspired by the legend

22

of the Tower of Babel and was called *Tit for Tat*.
He then wrote a burlesque opera, *The Girl of the
Golden Toothbrush*, for the Western Club. This
club brought together students from out West who
were determined to find a place for themselves at
Harvard. Reed joined and soon was presiding at
meals for the members in much the same way his
father had once presided at the Arlington Club. He
entertained everyone with his stories and thoroughly enjoyed himself with these young men
among whom he felt so much at home.

But "home" was never any one place for Reed,
not yet. Not only the writer in him but the youth
in him wanted to be everywhere and excluded from
nothing. Moreover his social and intellectual values
were in no way clearly defined. They were a contra-
dictory jumble from which at times a powerful
democratic instinct emerged, at times an envious
desire to belong to the privileged elite. He was far
from ready to choose one world of ideas at the
sacrifice of the possible rewards another might
offer.

On the one hand, he was an interested listener
at the sessions of the Socialist Club, which were
headed by his fellow student Walter Lippmann.
Reed was curious about the members' attacks on
the university for underpaying its servants, the
reform legislation they wanted passed by the
Massachusetts Legislature, and the efforts they
made at creating a league for woman suffrage. On

the other hand, he felt thoroughly comfortable as a college cheerleader, enjoying the heady sensation he experienced when he stood up before thousands of students in the bleachers. Too, when the Harvard aristocrats, desperate for a good lyric writer, swallowed their prejudices and asked Reed to join the Hasty Pudding Club, he did not refuse. He wrote the lyrics for a musical comedy they were producing, *Diana's Debut*, but he had not forgotten his rancor at these men as witnessed by one of the verses he inserted:

> *Just insist that your aunt was a Cabot,*
> *And your grandmother's real name was Weld.*
> *Try hard to make rudeness a habit,*
> *And be careful with whom you're beheld.*

The rancor persisted for, despite the fact that Reed had become president of the Western Club and a member of the editorial board of both the *Lampoon* and the *Monthly*, the fortress of the Harvard aristocrats still barred its gates against him, except when they needed a good lyric writer. While they occasionally accepted a few students from other social strata—as they later accepted his brother Harry—they recognized something in John Reed that they feared and distrusted. There was a rebellious, mocking streak which made them suspect that while he was making overtures to them out of one side of his mouth, he was laughing at them out of the other, that while he appeared to

24

respect them and what they stood for, fundamentally he held them in contempt. No matter how hard he tried to hide it, the defiant rebel in Reed always showed at the wrong time—in some strait-laced Back Bay drawing room, for instance, where he would shock his listeners by brashly expounding the ideals of free love, or by the deliberately rude way he treated influential people while being kind and considerate to "nobodies." The Harvard aristocrats were aware of something of which Reed himself was not, for he remained bewildered to the end by their rejection. He wanted to be accepted on his own terms, and he did not understand that they could only accept a man on *their* terms.

But if four years of Harvard did not make of Reed a member of the social elite, it did help to make a finer writer of him and this, in large measure, was due to an extraordinary professor, Charles Townsend Copeland, or "Copey," as he was familiarly called by decades of adoring undergraduates.

Copeland was not at all the conventional college don. He tried to awaken the intellectual curiosity of his students, to help them discover their genuine feelings, and then to learn to set them down with the clarity and beauty of language of which he himself had over many long and persistent years become a master. He took a deep personal interest in everyone in his class. He treated them as equals; he considered them his friends. His formal job was the teaching of English 12, but one could learn as

Charles Townsend Copeland

much if not more when one was invited to confer-
ences in his rooms at Hollis Hall. Copeland was a
showman and a scholar, an eccentric too among his
colleagues in that he was more at home in bars and

cafés than at their distinguished gatherings. He so clearly preferred the company of his students to anyone else's that he paid for these affronts to academic tradition by being kept an instructor for years, while infinitely less competent or inspired men rose to the rank of professor.

Copeland enjoyed one privilege, however, which was the right to select his students, and when Reed requested admittance to his course, Copeland at first refused. He had heard Reed was a troublesome element with a reputation for talking back to professors. But Reed had heard of Copeland too and his class was one rare opportunity which he was loath to pass up. He begged to be accepted, promising to behave properly, and Copeland at last consented. Neither the phenomenal teacher nor his eager student ever regretted the man's change of heart.

In fact, Copeland became one of the most powerful influences in Reed's life. He saw what no one else up to now had seen, that in this yearning, life-loving, rough-hewn boy from Oregon lurked a fine poet, a serious writer, perhaps even a genius. And perceiving this, he stimulated him "to find color and strength and beauty in books and in the world and to express it again." In the dedication to his former teacher in his first book, *Insurgent Mexico*, Reed acknowledged his debt when he said: "To listen to you is to learn how to see the hidden beauty of the visible world; to be your friend is to

Reed's many college activities were noted in the Harvard Class Album of 1910.

try to be intellectually honest." In *Almost Thirty* Reed noted: "There are two men who give me confidence in myself, who make me want to work, and to do nothing unworthy. . . ." One of them was Lincoln Steffens, who would later launch him in his career as a journalist; the other was his instructor in English 12.

In June of 1910 John Reed graduated from Harvard. His parents came East for the ceremony, C.J. interrupting a tight campaign for nomination as Republican candidate for Congressman and thus fatally undermining his chance to win. When his supporters had objected to his leaving Portland at this crucial stage, he had paid no heed. He had always had a determined dream that he would see any son of his through the finest university in the country and he had come to witness the fulfillment of that dream.

As John Reed sat in the packed stadium listening to the valedictory oration, his own dreams were already reaching far beyond the ivy-clad walls of the college campus, however. He scarcely heard the melodic singing of the Class Ode, written by one of his classmates, T. S. Eliot. He was listening to another voice inside him, which echoed the urgent advice he had received from Copey: he must see the world and he must write about it.

three:

After his graduation from Harvard, Reed came to his father with a plan to work his way across the Atlantic to Europe and from there, living on what he could earn from odd jobs and from writing about his travels, to continue on around the world. C.J. listened to what seemed a romantic, perhaps thoroughly unrealistic scheme and immediately approved of it. That was the sort of man C.J. was. He didn't want his son to move directly from school desk to office desk as he himself had done. He saw the soul of a poet in the boy and wanted him to have every opportunity for experiences that would deepen his understanding of human nature. After the failure of his campaign for Congress, C.J. was in financial straits, yet he drew from his dwindling resources a hundred dollars and a letter of credit which he forced John to take with him.

One early July morning, Reed and another Harvard man, Waldo Peirce, sailed on a cattleboat, the S.S. *Bostonian*, to work their way to Liverpool as bull pushers. Reed had met Peirce during his days on the *Lampoon* when Peirce, who later became a distinguished painter, was making a reputation for himself on campus with his clever cartoons. The son of a wealthy Maine family, Peirce could well have afforded passage on a luxury liner like the *Mauretania*, which could carry him in comfort and ease to Europe where he intended to study art. But Reed, looking forward to sharing the lives of the hardened seamen who would be their companions on the *Bostonian*, had been persuasively insistent that an artist ought to be familiar with other worlds than his own. Peirce grudgingly signed on.

The filthy, raffish steamboat with the seven hundred lowing steers it carried in its hold had hardly left Boston harbor, however, when Peirce sorely regretted his choice. A bowl of watery soup with white worms floating in it was set down before him, and he instantly threatened to dive overboard and swim back to the *Mauretania* which stood invitingly at her dock. Reed reminded him that he had signed the ship's articles, which meant that he was legally bound to carry on the voyage.

Yet as dawn rose after the first night at sea, Peirce could not be found. Had he actually carried out his threat? Reed was convinced of it, especially when he discovered Peirce's watch and wallet on his own bunk. The tough crew, however, held another view of the matter. It would not be the first time in their experience that a seaman had robbed another and pitched his body into the ocean. As for the captain, he made it plain that if Peirce did not show up at Liverpool to meet the boat, Reed would be brought before a board of inquiry to face a charge of murder.

Reed was not really worried—his friend would show up, he was certain. It was only out of the writer's habit he had already acquired that he jotted the episode down in a journal he was keeping on board ship. This first entry, along with subsequent entries inspired by later developments, would form the basis of a story called "Overboard" which would one day be published in the *Saturday Evening Post*. For the time being, however, he simply put the matter out of his mind and carried on with his job as bull pusher.

He had the care of a hundred cattle. He dragged heavy buckets of water to each of his charges twice a day, then hoisted hay until every joint in his body ached. He stood watch from eight in the evening till four in the morning. When the sea was high and the steers, roped in their crowded pens below, became frightened and dangerous, he had to tear around among flying hoofs and horns to recapture the ones which had broken loose. He was half-dead with exhaustion by the time he hit his bunk, after nibbling at a tin plateful of rotted food. But even then he could not sleep for the stench of rank clothing that filled the forecastle along with the rasping and drunken swearing of his bunk-mates.

There were ten other college men on board besides himself, and Reed organized them into a protest group. He argued that they were merely being given free passage, while the professional bull pushers were at least being paid to suffer. He insisted on their demanding better conditions, but the captain turned a deaf ear. Then Reed, with his eye on the cook and the mate, suggested a little bribery. Soon money changed hands and the young "gentlemen" began receiving the same food that was served at the officers' mess. What they came to call the "University Club" was installed in a tent in the open air on the poop deck. In addition the "gentlemen" were given special permission to take saltwater showers every afternoon.

But Reed, too curious to remain with one crowd alone, also struck up acquaintances with the professional bull pushers. One of them, he discovered, had been robbed of every cent just before he boarded ship. Reed took up a collection among his friends and gave it to the man. After that a lively sympathy for him developed among the seamen, especially the Irish contingent, who were seriously worried about his fate if the ship reached Liverpool and Peirce were not there to prove Reed's innocence. As they approached the coast of Ireland, they begged him to slip overboard and hide out in

Cork until they could help him. But the idea of being brought up on a murder charge seemed so preposterous to Reed that he gave no thought to their urgings.

When the *Bostonian* arrived at Liverpool, a tug was sent out to meet it. Reed, as he later wrote, searched for some sign of Waldo Peirce, but his friend was nowhere in sight. The captain, convinced of his guilt now, placed Reed in leg-irons and confined him to a small cabin below deck. He remained there all night while the boat worked its way up the Ship Canal to dock the next morning at Manchester. There his leg-irons were removed and Reed was walked down the gangplank behind the captain and flanked by two British policemen. They conducted him into a somber room of an official building where a board of inquiry was waiting to decide whether or not he should be put on trial for murder.

Reed's spirits were at a low ebb. The Irish sailors had warned him he would be convicted by British justice and hung from the nearest yardarm. But then the presumed "murder victim," refreshed from his pleasant crossing on the *Mauretania*, walked into the hearing room. Waldo Peirce had not shown up at Liverpool because he had consulted a lawyer who had advised him against it and with reason, for suddenly all the captain's wrath fastened on Peirce whom he demanded be charged with "maritime desertion." Peirce embroidered the facts of his disappearance by saying that he had become terribly seasick and had accidentally fallen overboard and if anyone should be charged it ought to be the captain for criminal negligence of the safety of his crew! Immense confusion followed, which resulted in nothing except the board of inquiry's helpless conclusion that they had been dealing with crazy Americans.

As the two "crazy Americans" walked out of the building, the rough band of cattlemen and sailors from the *Bostonian*, who had been anxiously awaiting the verdict, gave their friend Reed a rousing cheer, while Peirce was spared none of the colorful four-letter words in their vocabularies. It was not for Reed, however, and especially for the writer he was becoming, to put up complacently with anticlimaxes. He was determined now to make the rest of his trip, if not as dramatic as its start, at least as rewarding an experience. He tried to convince Peirce of the value of learning to know the English at close hand by traveling not as ordinary tourists but by hiking on foot through the countryside. Peirce, though, had had enough of Reed's bright ideas for "mingling with the people" and shook his head; he was going to the civilized city of London. So the two friends separated temporarily, and Reed went his own way.

He spent the next few weeks wandering wherever impulse led. With nothing but a pair of stout shoes and the rough clothing he wore on his back, he started off toward the Welsh mountains, taking in everything on the way, from beautiful pageants in lordly mansions to the country dances of farmers in small villages. He tramped over the countryside until his feet were covered with blisters and he had to stop to rest for a day, while "people came from miles around," he wrote his family, "to see the fool American who walked when he could ride."

Reed hiked as far as the Welsh border, then turned back toward Stratford-on-Avon where he planned to see Shakespeare's tomb. He arrived on a Sunday when the "No Admittance" sign was up, but by dodging the beadle and entering with the morning worshipers, he managed to reach the hallowed spot. He wanted to see Mervyn's Tower too, but when he arrived in Kenilworth on a rented bicycle, he discovered the tower closed as well—so he broke in.

In the middle of August, Reed returned to London to rejoin Waldo Peirce. The people of a country would always interest him more than its monuments, and it did not take Reed long to cover the sights of the city. With the money his father had provided, as well as money he earned by selling a couple of articles to the *London Daily News*, he bought himself new suits and shirts, a cutaway and a tuxedo, and he was ready to leave with Peirce for Paris.

But how should they travel? Reed suggested that they smuggle themselves across the Channel on a fishing boat. Peirce was irritated by his companion's urge to do things the hard way merely for the excitement of it or for the sake of the spectacular image of himself it created. He refused, insisting they pay their fares like normal people. Reed argued so persistently, however, that they compromised; instead of a fishing boat, they would stow away on a Channel steamer.

They were ignominiously caught in their hiding place on the boat and threatened with arrest. They talked their way out of it with the tame story that they had just found a friend on board who could pay for their tickets. But by this time Peirce's irritation had increased to such an extent that when they reached Calais, once again they separated and Reed went his own way—this time to the capital of France.

Paris—the City of Light, of bright cafes and dark adventure, of art, of beauty, of love—lived up perfectly to its reputation in Reed's eyes. One night he would emerge in cutaway and tie from the elegant red plush interior of Maxim's in the company of Harvard men from the Hasty Pudding Club, all singing his lyrics from their old shows at the top of their lungs. The next night, in dungarees and open shirt, he would be dancing the java with some pretty French barmaid at a neighborhood dance hall strung with colored bulbs and paper ribbons. The following evening he would be sitting in tweeds at a polite dinner across the table from

37

Professor Schofield of Harvard—who was in Paris lecturing at the Sorbonne—discussing the art and culture of the Old World.

Restless to see all, he was off again soon in a motor car with a bunch of Harvard boys and French girls, stopping at roadside hotels, or sleeping in the fields, or stripping to the skin to dive through the ocean waves on the beaches at midnight. The young crowd went to Le Havre for an aviation meet, dined and gambled in the casino, then drove southward again to catch the bullfights in San Sebastian.

Leaving his friends to return to Paris without him, Reed continued farther on into Spain. Without knowing a word of the language, he talked all the same, with his hands, with his eyes, striking up chance acquaintances wherever he could—in third-class trains, in run-down inns, or heat-baked plazas.

He went to Toledo, Burgos, Valladolid, Madrid. But, even when merely sightseeing, he displayed what Walter Lippmann later referred to as "an inordinate desire to be arrested." As he was changing trains at Medina del Campo, where a royal visitor was expected, the local police picked him up because they were under orders to remove from the scene anyone with the dangerous look of a Spanish anarchist. Reed, odd looking in the pair of dusty peasant corduroys he had bought himself in Spain, seemed to fit the description. He was soon released, however, when he proved to the authorities that he was an American citizen. Exhilarated by all he had seen, he made notes for an essay which he would later call "A Dash into Spain." Then, as autumn approached, he took a train back to Paris.

There a mood as somber and gray as the November skies overhead descended on him. He discovered with shock that he had hardly a cent left. Most of the family money, moreover, had evaporated— his frisky grandmother had managed to run heedlessly through a great fortune, so no help was to be looked for in that quarter. His father, who had done such a thorough job of exposing graft during his term as marshal that he was blackballed by the influential men he had attacked, was now trying none too successfully to sell insurance. Reed began to realize from the letters he received from home that C.J. had been making a painful sacrifice so that his older son might not miss a single pleasant experience abroad. Reed was writing stories and poems in his cheap hotel room, but his prospects for earning money in Paris were negligible. He began to reflect seriously now upon the wisdom of continuing his trip around the world. He would give himself two more months in Europe, he decided, and then go back home to find a job.

This decision was not bitter or grim. Reed would never be the sort of man who divided life down the middle, with one dark and dreary side representing Work and the other, bright and sunny side, Pleasure. Grandmother Green had always been ready for anything as long as she could find some excitement in it. For Reed, work and play, as long as they passionately engaged his interest, would always be equally absorbing.

Despite his lack of funds, he made the most of the time that remained to him in France. He explored the regions around Paris on several side trips from which he returned to set down his impressions. As Christmas drew near, he was overcome by a wave of nostalgia and wrote a poem for his mother which he spent several days carefully lettering and decorating by hand. Then he planned one more long trip before his departure, setting off alone for Avignon, Tarascon, Marseilles, and Toulon.

Reed did not remain alone for long, however. At Toulon he caught up with Waldo Peirce who was traveling with a group of friends, among whom were two sisters, nieces of a French scholar, Madeleine and Marguerite Filon. Reed joined them on a walking tour along the Mediterranean coast, during which he and Madeleine Filon spent a good deal of time together. When they reached Monte Carlo, Waldo Peirce, who had come to feel that nothing Reed could do would surprise him any longer, was surprised nevertheless when Reed suddenly announced joyously that he and Madeleine were engaged.

Reed was more determined than ever to hurry home now. He wanted to "make a million dollars" so that he could come back and marry Madeleine. He was thoroughly convinced he was in love with her, but somewhere too in his young writer's heart he knew that an engagement to a lovely French girl was a suitable romantic climax to a first trip abroad.

four:

Greenwich Village was the most logical place in America for John Reed to gravitate to when he returned from Europe. A little jungle of narrow winding streets far from the stately mansions and soaring office buildings of uptown Manhattan, the Village was notorious in the second decade of this century for the long-haired, poor, but aspiring artists and poets and writers who lived in its low-priced rooming houses. Men and women who had recently dwelt there had already made famous names for themselves in the literary world— Stephen Crane, Frank Norris, Willa Cather, and Theodore Dreiser. Reed was ambitious to join their ranks.

Before settling in the Village, however, he first paid a visit to Portland where he discovered the family finances to be even more precarious than he had suspected. Though his father was valiantly succeeding in putting John's brother Harry through

Harvard, C.J. was burdened with heavy debts and mortgages. Their older son was given a warm welcome, but he could not help but note his parents' dismay at the announcement that before long he expected to be able to support both himself and a wife. Fleeing their worried faces, he determinedly hastened East to prove himself.

Reed's romance with Madeleine Filon began to fade almost from the moment he arrived in New York, however, and before six months were out he wrote her and broke off their engagement. It was partly time and distance that made him realize he did not really care for her sufficiently. But it was also because he had fallen in love again—this time with a city. It was not a fickle love. It was a steady passion that took hold of Reed for life and he would never feel happy for long away from New York. In *Almost Thirty* he wrote:

> *New York was an enchanted city to me.... I wandered about the streets, from the soaring imperial towers of down-town, along the East River docks, smelling of spices and the clipper ships of the past, through the swarming East Side—alien towns within towns—where the smoky flare of miles of clamorous pushcarts made a splendor of shabby streets.... I spent all one summer night on top of a pier of the Williamsburg Bridge; I slept another night in a basket of squid in the Fulton Market, where*

*the red and green and gold sea things glisten in
the blue light of the sputtering arcs. . . . I found
wonderful obscure restaurants, where the foods
of the whole world could be found. I knew how
to get dope; where to go to hire a man to kill an
enemy; what to do to get into gambling rooms
and secret dance-halls. I knew well the parks,
and the streets of palaces, the theaters and
hotels; the ugly growth of the city spreading
north like a disease, the decrepit places whence
life was ebbing, and the squares and streets
where an old, beautiful leisurely existence was
drowned in the mounting roar of the slums. . . .
I went to gangsters' balls at Tammany Hall, on
excursions of the Tim Sullivan Association, to
Coney Island on hot summer nights. . . . Within
a block of my house was all the adventure in
the world; within a mile was every foreign
country.*

That he had come to love New York with eyes
which were quick to take in both its ugliness and
its grandeur was due in great part to the unusual
man who first introduced him to the metropolis—
a mild-mannered widower of forty-four, Lincoln
Steffens.

Steffens was a friend of John Reed's father. A
journalist by profession, he was above all known
as a "muckraker," his pen being the rake that dug
political muck out of secret places and exposed it.

Lincoln Steffens

45

His articles, along with his book *The Shame of the Cities*, had made him an admired figure in the radical community where people were protesting the social injustices of the day—the inhuman working conditions in the sweatshops and mines, the poverty caused by recurring economic crises, and the debasement of women classified with children and idiots through the denial to them of the right to vote.

Lincoln Steffens was acquainted with people of every political shading and was known for his almost saintly tolerance for any man's viewpoint, whether he agreed with it or not. Reed had met him during his days at Harvard but, as he later wrote of Steffens, "I was afraid of him then—afraid of his wisdom, his seriousness, and we didn't talk." Now, however, he was not only willing to talk but to listen, for it was obvious that Steffens could teach him a great deal. Reed's political knowledge, based primarily on what he had heard at meetings of the Socialist Club at college, was sketchy and haphazard. Steffens soon noted this and, not only out of friendship for C.J. but because he immediately warmed to the young man's sunny personality, he was more than ready to help Reed fill in the gaps in his education.

He took him along to meetings of Socialists, of anarchists, of single taxers, of labor leaders, and of what Reed called "all the hair-splitting Utopians and petty doctrine-mongers who cling to the skirts of Change." He sent him to Frank Shay's radical bookshop with a list of recommended reading. Above all, he urged him to go out into the city to explore it on his own. In this he showed an intuitive wisdom, for Reed was the sort of man who would always learn more from firsthand experience than from other men's words.

"I had to see," he remarked in *Almost Thirty.* "It didn't come to me from books. . . . In my rambles about the city I couldn't help but observe the ugliness of poverty and all its train of evil, the cruel inequality between rich people who had too many motor-cars and poor people who didn't have enough to eat."

Steffens not only helped reinforce in Reed a growing social consciousness, he also helped him find a job. First he secured him temporary work on a newspaper, the *New York Globe*, then a place on the staff of the *American Magazine*, which blended muckraking articles with popular fiction. Reed's task on the *American* was a routine one of correcting proof and reading manuscripts, but it was at least a beginning, and he was grateful. Steffens had already become for him that second great influence, after Copeland, who would make him "want to work and to do nothing unworthy."

Reed moved into an apartment at 42 Washington Square in Greenwich Village with three Harvard friends—Robert Andrews, Robert Rogers, and Alan Osgood. Andrews, a young man of acid wit who had been on the *Lampoon*, had taken a job in advertising. Robert Rogers, who had been on the *Monthly*'s staff and who now worked for the *Brooklyn Eagle*, was ambitious not only for himself but for Reed, whom he constantly nagged with his slogan *nulla dies sine linea*—never let a day go by without writing a line. Alan Osgood, another ex-editor of the *Lampoon*, was the one whose company Reed enjoyed the most because of "his unfailing laughter and kindness." These four formed the nucleus of a crowd of Harvard men who drifted in and out of 42 Washington Square. One day Alan Seeger would arrive and, if no one was at home, slip his latest poem under the door. Walter Lippmann, whom Steffens had helped find a job on a magazine called *Everybody's*, was a frequent visitor, and later on there was the lean, hungry stage designer, Robert Edmond Jones.

Reed grew so fond of Steffens that he cajoled the lonely widower into moving into the same building on the floor below. Steffens was happy to be there, though Reed never left him in peace. He would burst into Steffens's room in the middle of the night to wake him out of a sound sleep. He would tell him about some marvelous experience he had had that evening or some new and amazing person he had just encountered—a drunk in the Bowery, a sailor off a foreign ship, a prostitute with an absolutely unbelievable life story. Steffens would listen sympathetically and only when it seemed that

Walter Lippmann

Reed would never stop would the older man inter-
rupt and advise him to write it all down.

Reed, of course, wanted nothing better than to
write it all down, but during his first year in New

York, no one paid much attention to the young man who sat with his blue pencil at an obscure desk at the *American*. No one paid any attention either to the manuscripts he had brought back from Europe or the new ones he was producing. In fact, often the only real evidence he had of his existence as a writer was a special file he kept, labeled "Posthumous and Juvenile Works of J. S. Reed, Bart.," which contained the poems and stories he had sent off to various magazines—and their accompanying rejection slips.

He was trying to laugh off his first defeats, as he had laughed off defeats before. He submitted and resubmitted, he wrote and rewrote stories until at times he didn't know whether he was improving them or simply making them worse. But he was determined and energetic, and at last his efforts began to bring results.

He was asked to do a column for a new department the *American* had instituted called "Interesting People" and wrote a glowing piece on Charles Townsend Copeland. Then, with an already established writer, Julian Street, he reworked a story he had based on his cattleboat experience and, under their joint signature, "Overboard" was printed in the *Saturday Evening Post*. Another story of his, "The Man from the Seine," sat gathering dust in editorial offices for a year until finally, with some revision, it appeared in *Century*. "Showing Mrs. Van" turned up on the pages of the *Smart Set*.

Then there was an editorial, "Immigrants," which found its way into *Collier's,* an essay, "The Involuntary Ethics of Big Business," taken by *Trend,* and a poem of his, "The Wanderer to His Heart's Desire," which was set to music by Arthur Foote.

Reed was beginning to feel like a professional writer and was beginning to be regarded as one too. He was invited to join the Dutch Treat Club—an organization of successful men of arts and letters which had sprung up in New York and which counted among its members writers like Rupert Hughes, the humorist Irvin S. Cobb, and the artist and illustrator James Montgomery Flagg. Copey asked Reed up to Harvard to deliver a lecture on writing to the students of English 12. Above all, Reed was beginning to be talked of in literary circles around the city as "a coming man."

His parents were more than pleased. His father wrote him, "I think and talk of you every day and love and am proud of you every hour."

Toward the end of June 1912, a telegram brought Reed the sudden news that his father was critically ill. The burden of financial worries, which he had sought to conceal beneath a facade of unflagging good humor, had utterly broken C.J.'s health. Reed hastened to Portland to spend sad silent hours at his father's bedside until C.J. died on a morning in early July.

Reed was deeply affected. It seemed to him that only now did he fully appreciate the sacrifices C.J.

had made so that he and his brother could be educated in the style of rich men's sons. The interest in the radical movement which Steffens had fostered in him gave Reed a deeper appreciation too of the crusade his father had led against political corruption during his days as marshal. Reed felt a growing determination to take part in the crusades of his own day, and he was impatient to return to New York.

He was obliged, however, to remain in Portland for the next three months in order to help his mother straighten out the family affairs. Still, during that time, he could not help but think longingly of life in Greenwich Village. He recalled the night romps he and his roommates had indulged in, dodging in and out of doorways along the narrow streets, chasing each other like schoolboys. He remembered the long evenings they had spent in cheap neighborhood resturants, scribbling poems or drawings on the tabletops, while they filled the air with impassioned discussions. He remembered, too, how others had sometimes complained of the exaggerated high spirits of "Storm Boy" Reed and of how little heed he had given to such complaints. To him Village life was a manifestation of a beautiful freedom from constraint. It was a defiance of convention and a liberation from the bonds a standardized society sought to impose.

In a long poem which he wrote during his stay in Portland, he tried to capture the flavor of that life.

The poem was called *The Day in Bohemia, or Life Among the Artists*, and it was dedicated to Lincoln Steffens with these lines:

Steffens, I hope I am doing no wrong to you
By dedicating this doggerel song to you;
P'raps you'll resent
The implied compliment,
But light-hearted Liberty seems to belong to you.

In the poem Reed described twenty-four hours in the existence of the four Harvard men who lived in the third floor rear, where:

In winter the water is frigid,
In summer the water is hot;
And we're forming a club for controlling the tub
For there's only one bath to the lot.
You shave in unlathering Croton,
If there's water at all, which is rare,—
But the life isn't bad for a talented lad
At Forty-Two Washington Square!

The dust it flies in at the window,
The smells they come in at the door,
Our trousers lie meek where we threw 'em last week
Bestrewing the maculate floor.
The gas isn't all that it should be,
It flickers,—and yet I declare
There's pleasure or near it for young men of spirit
At Forty-Two Washington Square!

53

But nobody questions your morals,
And nobody asks for the rent,—
There's no one to pry if we're tight, you and I,
Or demand how our evenings are spent.
The furniture's ancient but plenty,
The linen is spotless and fair,
O life is a joy to a broth of a boy
At Forty-Two Washington Square!

It was true that the young men who came to 42 Washington Square longed to serve Art and couldn't without starving, so they scrounged for a living writing advertising or correcting proof or drawing pictures for clothing catalogues. Yet . . .

Yet we are free who live in Washington Square,
We dare to think as Uptown wouldn't dare,
Blazing our nights with arguments uproarious;
What care we for a dull world censorious
When each is sure he'll fashion something glorious?

Each was sure he would fashion something glorious, and not the least of them, Reed. But *when?* he asked himself impatiently. And he asked this "when?" more and more often after his return to New York, as he began to feel the urge to see something of his in print which had more significance than the skillful but conventional articles and stories he had been turning out for the popular magazines.

This impatience came not simply from a desire

to find a special and unique place as a writer. It came from a need to express his feelings about what he was observing around him. He wanted to give voice to the suffering of the anonymous "nobodies" he had met on his walks through the city—a peddler in the streets making an impoverished living selling "Matrimonial News" for a nickel to passersby; a girl in a cheap dance hall in the Haymarket, selling her youth and beauty to any man who came along. He had already written stories about such people and he would write many more, but nobody wanted them. They went the rounds of all the magazines, but always came back to him, rejected. They were not amusing or distracting, he was told; they would not please weary readers who sought to forget rather than be reminded of the troubles of the world; they were not suitable material, moreover, to be found lying about a home where innocent children's eyes might fall upon them.

His poetry fared somewhat better. *Everymagazine, an Immorality Play*, for which he wrote the lyrics, had been performed to great acclaim at the annual gathering at Delmonico's of the Dutch Treat Club. *The Day in Bohemia* and *Sangar*, another long poem also dedicated to Steffens, earned him praise from eminent contemporaries, Edwin Arlington Robinson, Louis Untermeyer, and Harriet Monroe. Still, he was forced to print most of his poetry privately, paying all the costs himself.

55

He was facing a dilemma to which at first he saw
no solution. He wanted to express his convictions
with no regard for demands other than those of
intellectual honesty and artistic integrity. But at
the same time, he had to earn his living by writing.
As Reed himself put it:

> *How can an artist create his Utopia*
> *With his best eye on the World's cornucopia?*

Before long he discovered in New York, however,
as he had discovered at Harvard, that he was not
alone. Other artists were facing the same dilemma
and, moreover, were beginning to do something
about it. They were creating a magazine of their
own, *The Masses*.

The *Masses* had existed since early in 1911 as an
organ in part devoted to the cooperative aspects of
the Socialist movement, in part to muckraking articles, and in part to European fiction. It had never
possessed any sharply defined direction, however,
and was foundering financially. When Reed heard
of it in the autumn of 1912, it was being reorganized
—under the editorship of Max Eastman, a former
instructor in aesthetics at Columbia—to meet the
growing need for an outlet for radical writing as
well as for art and fiction which could not find a
place in the commercial magazines.

Reed appeared one day at the *Masses*' downtown
offices with a story called "Where the Heart Is," a

The offices of the Masses *in Greenwich Village as depicted by one of the magazine's artists, Glenn Coleman.*

APRIL, 1913　　　　10 CENTS

The MASSES

HIGH COST
OF LIVING

RAISE IN WAGES

APRIL FOOL

A STORY BY LINCOLN STEFFENS IN THIS NUMBER

tale about the sad and bitter life of a dance hall
girl. It had been rejected time and again by the
uptown magazines for its uncompromising realism.

Eastman immediately accepted it, however, and accepted Reed along with it, not only as a contributor but as a member of the editorial staff. Reed even had a part in formulating the magazine's new creed which was to print "what is too naked or true for the money-making press," to take a stand "against rigidity and dogma" and to do "what it pleases and conciliate nobody, not even its readers."

As the magazine grew, Reed found himself working side by side with some of the leading literary and artistic talents of his day—artists like John Sloan, Art Young, and George Bellows, poets like Arturo Giovannitti, Louis Untermeyer, and Harry Kemp. Over the years Carl Sandburg, Sherwood Anderson, Bertrand Russell, Vachel Lindsay, and Maxim Gorky were among the magazine's contributors.

The *Masses* could not afford to pay its writers anything at all, yet Reed drew from it something more valuable to him than money. It mattered less now that he was forced to earn his living by fashioning tailor-made stories for the paying magazines uptown, when in the columns of this downtown magazine he could write as he chose. Even more importantly, the freedom of expression offered by the *Masses* opened up a new direction to his career, one which had always intrigued him and which would be decisive for his future—journalism.

five:

Reed was not long in finding an important story to cover as a journalist, though he fell upon it by chance. He had attended many meetings where leaders of the left-wing labor movement spoke from public platforms, but through Steffens and his contacts on the *Masses*, he had begun to meet some of those leaders personally as well. One evening he was invited to Bill Haywood's apartment in lower Manhattan.

Haywood—or "Big Bill," as he was known to thousands of laboring men throughout the country —was a man of imposing stature, with one blind eye and one coal black one. A Socialist and a leader of the International Workers of the World, his ultimate aim in life was the ultimate aim of the I.W.W. —to see that workers throughout the world enjoyed the full fruit of their labor instead of giving up a large part of it in profits to their employers. That was a dream for the future, however. The

60

immediate aim of the I.W.W. was to organize not only the skilled workers the American Federation of Labor was also trying to organize, but all workers including the unskilled, from every American factory and mill and mine, into an O.B.U., or One Big Union. I.W.W. organizers like Haywood had been traveling throughout the United States in recent years urging laborers to strike for decent wages, proper working conditions, an eight-hour day. These were demands every American worker now considers fundamental. But in Reed's time, the men and women who made such demands were considered by many to be criminals, dangerous agitators, even traitors to their country.

That evening at Haywood's, Reed was part of a small informal gathering of people sitting on the floor or on the few available sticks of furniture in the bare, candlelit room. Among them was the woman who lived with Bill Haywood and who taught in a New York high school. Hutchins Hapgood, a journalist who wrote for the *Globe*, was present with his wife, Neith. There were a few others whom Reed did not know, including a woman in crimson who resembled a sphinx in the wise glint of her quiet eyes, in the whisper of a smile which seemed to play about her lips. In the beginning Reed was struck by her, wondering who she was, but then Haywood started to speak.

Big Bill talked about conditions in Paterson, New Jersey, where some twenty-five thousand silkworkers were striking for an eight-hour day. The strike had been dragging on for more than two months. Men had been thrown in jail on false charges, women had been beaten bloody by policemen's truncheons, and an Italian worker called Modestino had been shot dead by one of the factory owner's hired gunmen. Yet, surprisingly enough, virtually no one in New York knew about the Paterson strike, and Haywood blamed the press. The big city newspapers, in collaboration with the owners of the Paterson silk mills, had been engaged from the start in a calculated conspiracy of silence. They refused to print a word about the strikers, who were in desperate need of funds and moral support.

Unlike Big Bill, Reed had never been beaten up nor jailed nor persecuted. But his sympathy was genuine and he grasped the seriousness of what Haywood was saying. So did the others in the room. It was clear that the story of the Paterson strikers ought to be forced into the columns of the New York newspapers. But how? At this point the woman in crimson spoke up. Her voice was soft, almost timid, but what she suggested was bold and imaginative—to build a pageant around the story of the strike and to bring the strikers to New York to perform it themselves on the stage at Madison Square Garden.

The others were intrigued by the proposal but bewildered by its scope. How could you bring thou-

62

sands of workers to New York? How could you turn them, illiterate immigrants for the most part, into actors overnight? And, above all, who would organize, create, and produce such a pageant...?

Reed enthusiastically offered his services. He wrote down the woman's name—Mabel Dodge—and her address, 23 Fifth Avenue, and promised to visit her soon; they would produce the pageant together. But first he intended to do a reportage on the Paterson strike and somehow to see it into print.

Before dawn the next day, Reed took a train for Paterson, New Jersey, where at six o'clock in the morning he found the gray streets deserted beneath a light, cold rain. But as he headed toward the mill district, he saw at least twenty policemen strolling along with their nightsticks under their arms. Then he began to observe workmen going in the same direction, coat collars turned up, hands in their pockets. He came to a long street, one side of which was lined with tenements, the other side with silk mills, and there he noticed men and women laughing and chatting in doorways and windows, as if after breakfast on a holiday. As he later wrote:

There seemed to be no sense of expectancy, no strain or feeling of fear. The sidewalks were almost empty, only over in front of the mills a few couples—there couldn't have been more than fifty—marched slowly up and down, drip-

ping with the rain. Some were men, with here and there a man and woman together, or two young boys. As the warmer light of full day came, the people drifted out of their houses and began to pace back and forth, gathering in little knots on the corners. They were quick with gesticulating hands, and low-voiced conversation. They looked often toward the corners of side streets.

Suddenly appeared a policeman, swinging his club. "Ah-hh-h!" said the crowd softly.

Six men had taken shelter under the canopy of a saloon. "Come on! Get out of that!" yelled the policeman, advancing. The men quietly obeyed. "Get off this street! Go on home, now! Don't be standing there!" They gave way before him in silence, drifting back again when he turned away. Other policemen materialized, hustling, cursing, brutal, ineffectual. No one answered back. Nervous, bleary-eyed, unshaven, these officers were worn out with nine weeks' incessant strike duty.

On the mill side of the street the picket-line had grown to about four hundred. Several policemen shouldered roughly among them, looking for trouble. A workman appeared, with a tin pail, escorted by two detectives. "Boo! Boo!" shouted a few scattered voices. Two Italian boys leaned against the mill fence and shouted a merry Irish threat: "Scab! Come

64

outa here I knocka you' block off!" A police-
man grabbed the boys roughly by the shoulder.
"Get the hell out of here!" he cried, jerking
and pushing them violently to the corner,
where he kicked them. Not a voice, not a move-
ment from the crowd.

A little further along the street we saw a
young woman with an umbrella, who had been
picketing, suddenly confronted by a big police-
man.

"What the hell are you doing here?" he
roared. "God damn you, you go home!" and he
jammed his club against her mouth.

"I no go home!" she shrilled passionately,
with blazing eyes . . .

Silently, steadfastly, solidly the picket-line
grew. In groups or in couples the strikers pa-
trolled the sidewalk. There was no more laugh-
ing.

Up until now Reed had been merely a spectator,
but in the moments that followed, he became an
involuntary participant. It had begun to rain heav-
ily and he obtained a man's permission to stand on
the porch of his house. There was a policeman before him and Reed had to walk around him to
mount the steps. Suddenly the policeman swung
about and asked the owner if all the men on the
porch lived in the house. As Reed reported it:

The man indicated the three other strikers and himself, and shook his head at me.

"Then you get the hell out of here!" said the cop, pointing his club at me.

"I have the permission of this gentleman to stand here," I said. "He owns this house."

"Never mind! Do what I tell you! Come off of there, and come off damn quick!"

"I'll do nothing of the sort."

With that he leaped up the steps, seized my arm, and violently jerked me to the sidewalk. Another cop took my arm and they gave me a shove.

Not long afterwards, Reed found himself stripped of his possessions, wearing prison garb and being led toward the "convicted cell" in the Passaic County jail. He had been sentenced to twenty days for being insolent to a policeman. In the cell, a man driven mad by years of incarceration was shrieking at the top of his lungs. A syphilitic was sucking on a sugar pill which the prison doctor, diagnosing his illness as "nervousness," had prescribed. A seventeen-year-old boy, who had never been sentenced, paced up and down in a daze; he had not seen the sun for over nine months. And there were others in a similar plight in the vermin-infested cell, stinking of open toilets and rotten food.

During Reed's first few minutes as a prisoner, he discovered that it was not going to be easy to get the story he had come to Paterson to report. Among his forty-odd cellmates were fourteen strikers. The man who interested Reed most of all, however, was one he had seen on several occasions at political gatherings, if only from a distance, and he instantly recognized the high forehead and intense eyes of the fiery Italian strike leader Carlo Tresca. Tresca was talking to another prisoner, explaining the principles of class struggle. Reed approached the two and, with his usual candor, tried to join the discussion. Tresca became instantly suspicious. When Reed began to ply him with questions about the history of the strike, the Italian fell silent. The other strikers, taking their cue from Tresca and wary of the danger of a labor spy in their midst, followed suit.

All that night not a single striker spoke to Reed, and he ended up in a corner of the cell, staring at a tin plate of food that was worse than anything he had been handed even on the cattleboat. When he reached for the salt, hoping that it would cover the taste of the rotting meat, he found that there were bugs in it.

The next morning, however, Reed was liberated, if not from the prison, at least from his isolation, when Haywood was led into the cell. Big Bill, who had just been arrested without charge, greeted Reed warmly. He assured the others that Reed was trustworthy—they could speak freely before him. Tresca apologized for his coolness the night before, but Reed was already busy asking questions. . . .

Throughout the next few days and nights the strikers were continuously clustered about him. Sitting on the cell floor, he listened as they told him how they had been arrested, many of them, for walking peaceably up and down in front of the mill and been summarily charged with "unlawful assemblage." They told him about others who had been strolling back to their houses only to be grabbed by the police, clubbed and herded into patrol wagons on the charge of "rioting." They had all refused to ask for bail. Even if the money could have been raised, they didn't want it. They knew the jail could only hold so many men and, when too many were arrested, some would have to be let out—and then they could go straight back to the picket line.

Sometimes their talk would be interrupted when a new group of arrested strikers would be led into the cell. They would come in defiantly, singing the songs they had been singing on the picket line— "The Marseillaise" or "The International" or others whose words they had made up themselves about the strike and its leaders.

Once their talk was interrupted too when someone came in to announce that friends had offered to pay the fine for Reed's release. Reed shook his head—just let them send cigarettes and food. He didn't want to leave the jail. He was not only getting the story he was after but he was living with the people who were making it. He was experiencing for the first time what he had only read about or heard about from others. Roughed up by a policeman and thrown into jail to share, even temporarily, the same bitter lot as the strikers, he felt not only a sympathy for their cause but a sense of solidarity with them.

The strikers, for their part, were quick to respond to Reed's attitude. Heretofore they had regarded journalists with a deep-seated distrust. But this man seemed different from the others. The newspapers had never once told their side of any story but only the side of the employers, of the city officials, of the police. At last, in John Reed, they had found a voice.

"When it came time for me to go out," Reed wrote, "I said goodbye to all those gentle, alert, brave men, ennobled by something greater than themselves. . . . They crowded around me, patting my shoulder, my hand, friendly, warm-hearted, trusting, eloquent. . . ."

Reed had been released after only four days. The millowners, the New Jersey police, and the prison authorities had had more than enough of him. Indignant items about his imprisonment had sprouted up in the newspapers. And these powerful men bitterly admitted that the jailing of "one lousy Harvard poet" had done something that twenty-five thousand striking silkworkers had been unable to do; it had broken the wall of silence the press

69

had imposed on the strike. Paterson, New Jersey, could no longer be ignored, and soon the New York newspapers were beginning to give the strike extensive coverage.

Reed did his own story about it for the *Masses*. "War in Paterson" colorfully brought to life the struggles of the people involved and the political forces at work behind the scenes. It instantly marked Reed as a journalist of rare talent. More than ever his colleagues began to speak of him as "a coming man."

Reed himself, though delighted by the favorable reaction to his article, was almost too busy to savor it. He was already at work on new articles. Besides, he had not forgotten his promise to stage a pageant about the strike in Madison Square Garden, and one of the first people he went to see after his return to New York was that interesting woman-in-crimson—Mabel Dodge.

six:

Mabel Dodge was a rebel, but a rebel with an ample bank account. She lived in a luxurious apartment at 23 Fifth Avenue where the dazzling white of walls, of woodwork, and of flowing silk drapes were as much a defiance of the dirt and grime of New York as Mrs. Dodge herself was a defiance of all that was straitlaced and Victorian. She did not allow anything or anyone to restrict her independence, not even her husband of whom she was fond but whom she banished from her life for long intervals whenever she felt he was hindering her development. She wanted to live as she chose, travel where she chose, see whom she liked; a new freedom for women was in the air in those days and she considered herself a Modern Woman. Unorthodoxy was not only a hobby in her life but a passion, a principle.

It was Mabel Dodge, for instance, who first publicized the tradition-shattering writing of Gertrude

Mabel Dodge

Stein in America. It was she who helped organize
the famous Armory Show, which shocked and
stunned New York with the first examples of
Cubist art Americans had ever seen. But this shy

yet magnetic and intuitive woman in her early thirties was noted, above all, for her "Evenings," when she would collect in her salon people of every class and point of view, from highly respectable men and women of arts and letters to anarchists. She would set them to talking and arguing, while she sat quietly and enjoyed the heated debates. Afterwards hot tempers would be soothed when the butler, Vittorio, would throw open the dining room doors to reveal a sumptuous display of food.

Mabel Dodge did not hold these Evenings only for her own amusement but because she felt they were important—as indeed they were, for they provided a forum where people who would normally not come in contact with one another had the benefit of a free exchange of ideas. If the social elite of New York looked with dismay upon her unconventional ways, Mabel Dodge could not have cared less, for an infinitely more fascinating elite, in her eyes, the intellectual elite, moved in and out of her salon the year around—the poets Amy Lowell and Edwin Arlington Robinson; the sculptor Jo Davidson and the painter John Marin; the pioneer of the Birth Control movement, Margaret Sanger; Lincoln Steffens, Walter Lippmann, and countless others.

Forgotten, however, were all of them the day Reed arrived, ready to begin work on the pageant. As they exchanged ideas, he and Mrs. Dodge discovered an instant rapport, for nothing either one of them suggested seemed to the other too daring or too extreme. Madison Square Garden took up a whole city block; it was big enough to hold Barnum and Bailey's Circus with three rings and two bands going at once, but they would fill it. To get a performance out of more than a thousand silkworkers who spoke half a dozen different languages was an almost impossible feat, but they would accomplish it. It would cost a small fortune to rent the Garden even for one night, but they would raise the money. ... The fact that a spectacle of the sort they were envisioning had never been undertaken anywhere before presented a challenge to which something in both their bold natures responded.

A committee was quickly formed to plan and finance the production of the pageant, and meetings were held at Margaret Sanger's home. It was decided that Mabel would offer ideas and raise the money. Reed would write the scenario for the evening's program and train and rehearse the strikers. Robert Edmond Jones—who was later to pursue a brilliant career on Broadway as a stage designer, but who was then known to Reed only as the talented "Bobby," one of his former classmates at Harvard—would handle the scenery. Others would help in any way they could, even to the extent of going to flower shops and asking for donations of red carnations to be used during the reenactment of the funeral of Modestino, the striker who had been killed.

Reed quit his job on the *American* to devote his full time to the pageant. Working day and night, sleeping little and even then in his clothes, he ran back and forth between Paterson and New York. He and the strikers together created scenes for the pageant. Reed led them in songs they knew, like "Solidarity Forever" or "John Golden and the Lawrence Strike," the latter composed by Joe Hill, the famous labor organizer, for striking textile workers in Lawrence, Massachusetts. But Reed also made up songs of his own, setting new incendiary lyrics to the time-honored tune of "Harvard, Old Harvard!"

Throughout this period the Paterson strike continued and a mass meeting of thirty thousand people was held one Sunday in Haledon, a nearby town, because the right of assembly had been denied the strikers in their own city. Hutchins Hapgood described it, and Reed's participation in it, in his column in the *Globe:*

> *I never saw a more touching and beautiful sight. From an elevated position I could see the faces of men, women and children looking up to the speakers, who stood on the balcony of a house. They were thinking of things of the greatest importance to them, and indeed, to the whole of society, and their sensitive, expressive and tired faces responded to their emotions . . .*

75

*When John Reed, the young poet, and ener-
getic organizer of the pageant to be given by
the strikers in Madison Square Garden, led
them in the songs that they are to sing as they
march to New York, and on the picket lines in
Paterson, when his youthful, enthusiastic face
looked out over the sea of humanity beneath
him, and that mass of humanity responded in
rhythm, with deep, unconscious felicity and
grace and love of love and love of life, it was
to me a spectacle that I have never seen rivaled
on the stage.*

But during the preparations for the pageant,
Reed did not forget that he was a journalist. His
constant visits to Paterson reminded him of the
four days he had spent in the Passaic County jail
and of the appalling conditions there. Out of this
recollection came an article—"Sheriff Radcliff's
Hotel." Though the piece dealt with harsh social
truths, it was done in a satirical style palatable to
a broad reading public, and it occurred to Reed
that it just might go over with one of the big uptown magazines. He decided to try the *Metropolitan.*

The *Metropolitan* was a popular, expensively
printed and illustrated periodical of the day. It had
the rare reputation among slick magazines of taking into its pages writing of the first quality, with
a staggering array of literary stars among its contributors—George Bernard Shaw, D. H. Lawrence,

76

Joseph Conrad, H. G. Wells, Arnold Bennett, Rudyard Kipling, Edna Ferber, Fannie Hurst, Rupert Hughes, F. Scott Fitzgerald, and many others. At the same time it was sufficiently sensitive to the radical currents of its era to print pieces on social reform and even on socialism itself. It was an oddity, yet it existed. Reed slipped the manuscript into an envelope. After all, what had he to lose except the price of a stamp?

A few days later Carl Hovey, the editor of the *Metropolitan*, drew Reed's article from a pile of unsolicited manuscripts on his desk. When he saw that it was a reportage on prison conditions, he expected the usual grim treatment such subjects seemed always to require and he prepared himself for a boring quarter of an hour. Almost instantly, however, he found himself surprised and delighted by the originality of the author's approach.

It was true Reed had not failed to indicate in his article that the jail was of no use either to the human beings cast like refuse into its misery or to society. It was true too that he had found, in the white prisoners' bitter jokes and in the half-starved black men kneeling on the cold floor avidly watching a race between cockroaches, a magnificent proof of the indestructibility of the human spirit. And yet he had covered the Paterson institution and the sheriff who ran it with raillery, mingling anger with jest in a way that subtly yet inevitably got under the reader's skin.

Carl Hovey did not know at the time that this was but the first of many articles from the same writer which would reach his editorial desk, nor that it would mark the beginning of a fruitful association over the coming years between Reed, himself, and the *Metropolitan*. But as he wrote decades later, in his reminiscences, about the first work of John Reed's which had fallen into his hands:

> *In all this it was impossible to miss the presence of an untrammeled spirit ever so happily engaged. The bursting energy, the continuous flow, the straight look at his material—such qualities were new. With the joy that is the enticing reward of editorial servitude I clutched the manuscript and spoke for the future work of the author, all on a breath, knowing that what this boy had to offer was as far from being a pale copy of that past master in the field, Stephen Crane, as it was from bearing the slightest resemblance to the "picturesque" reporting then in vogue. Such writing was like the sweep of a sudden wind come to shake the closed windows of the literary scene out of their frames. Behold a new man! The light of a fresh, God-given talent was shining forth.*

Not long after, Reed stood in the editorial office of the *Metropolitan* while Hovey, as the latter recorded, observed the way he seemed to prefer to remain on his feet while he listened or talked—

78

Carl Hovey

though in the beginning he did not talk much and Hovey saw only a pale, intent face in the midst of what appeared to him a sunny silence. Then Reed said:

"You've got to think this over, I suppose."

"No."

Reed glanced up with surprise as Hovey went on, "I think it's great. I'm crazy about it."

"It's partly a josh," Reed began modestly. "I mean it, though," he added.

The talk turned to technical matters—about the article and about the date of its publication. But before they parted, the editor and the author spoke briefly of what made for good writing. It was a subject rendered important to them by the very same man. Though more than a decade separated them, both had sat at the feet of the inspired professor who roomed in Hollis Hall and both had come to revere Charles Townsend Copeland and his untiring devotion to literature.

Reed must have written a great deal, Hovey remarked, to have acquired such sureness, such a seemingly effortless flow. "You tell all," he said, "yet you know exactly where to stop, when too much would only bore the reader."

Reed responded instantly, "I know what you mean. I'm glad you think I can do it. Sometimes I think that what you leave out suggests more than what you actually say."

After Reed had gone, his face lingered long in Hovey's memory:

It was a young face very full of charm, it gave out the joy of life that churned within; yet undoubtedly the pale eyes could be furious. The unconscious defiance of the set of his head was like a mainspring of courageous action. There was an abounding assurance that was yet so natural and contradicted by modesty that it lacked all unpleasantness. . . .

I caught myself thinking, he does not look like Harry Kemp, or Upton Sinclair, or Vachel Lindsay, or Carl Sandburg, yet he reminds one of all of them. It must be because he belongs to their species, the new Democrats, who were shouting truths filled with sustenance concerning their fellow men.

Reed felt triumphant over the acceptance of his article by the *Metropolitan*. It appeared he had stumbled upon a way of writing which would enable him not only to express his own convictions on the pages of the *Masses*, but also to sell those convictions to the paying magazines. A new vista in his career seemed to be opening before him. He was deeply and sincerely involved in the cause of the Paterson strike and he never wanted to give up causes like it or give up writing about them; such writing satisfied the longing in him to do all he could toward improving the lot of humanity. At the same time, an equally passionate and youthful longing was lodged in him for glory, money, fame. With the *Metropolitan's* new interest in him, it now seemed possible—without in any way betraying his own integrity—for him to enjoy the best of both worlds.

Reed went back to work on the pageant with renewed enthusiasm. On June 17, 1913, over a thousand strikers left Paterson, New Jersey, in a fourteen-car special train. They got off at Hoboken and, by way of the ferries, reached New York where they marched up Fifth Avenue, with the International Workers of the World band in their lead, toward Madison Square Garden.

That night fifteen thousand spectators thronged the Garden. Working men and women came not only from Paterson but from all over the eastern states, and New York swelled their numbers with sympathizers. As the spectacle began with the sharp blast of a factory whistle, a hush came over the audience and all eyes turned toward the stage where hundreds upon hundreds of shrouded figures moved toward a building, stark and sinister under the glow of Bobby Jones's backlighting, and were swallowed up inside it... the mill. The whistle shrieked again, followed by the din of machinery; then all sounds died away to give place to the singing of "The Marseillaise," as the workers surged out of the factory in the first rays of dawn, and with one voice declared the strike on.

This was "Episode 1" of the scenario in which John Reed, during several stirring hours that night, traced the story of the ten-week long struggle of the Paterson strikers. By the time the coffin of Modestino, the Italian worker who had been shot during the early days of the strike, was borne from the back of the Garden on a ramp toward the stage and each striker dropped a red carnation on it as it passed slowly by, the invisible barrier between performer and spectator had long since dissolved and the entire audience was caught up in the dramatic days reenacted before them. Without realizing it, those present were assisting at the birth in America of a new art form, though the term "living newspaper" had not yet been invented.

The next day the press hailed the pageant as "a spectacular production" which had "established a legitimate form of 'demonstration' before which all others must pale." On Reed's work they commented that the "scenes unrolled with a poignant realism that no man who saw them will ever forget." They noted, too, that it was doubtful if Madison Square Garden had ever held, even during the bitterest of political campaigns, a larger audience than had packed it for the Paterson pageant.

Soon the journalists, initially so carried away by the spectacle that they had forgotten their papers' editorial policy, would have to rewrite their enthusiasm into niggling criticism, not of the artistic side of the pageant but of the "seditious" motives of the I.W.W. But by that time the Paterson workers were already back on the picket line striving with new heart to win their strike, while the originators of the pageant—Mabel Dodge and John Reed—were far away, sailing, with their brilliant stage designer, Robert Edmond Jones, on an ocean liner for Europe.

With money that a group of friends who believed

in his talent had collected, Jones was en route to Germany to study with the eminent theatre director Max Reinhardt. Reed, on the edge of a nervous collapse from his around-the-clock exertions on the pageant, had been invited by Mabel to spend the summer in her villa in Florence. Though hardly a word of a personal nature had passed between them during their close collaboration on the pageant, "we had taken for granted the inevitability of our love for each other," Mabel Dodge wrote many years later in the volume of her *Intimate Memories* called *Movers and Shakers*. Now, on shipboard, "we were free and ready to turn to each other. But, strangely, something in me resisted him strongly ... something in me adored the high clear excitement of continence, and the tension we had known together that came from our canalized vitality." And Mabel refused Reed's advances, even when they arrived under her stateroom door at midnight in the form of supplicating poetry.

In Paris, however, from where they planned to motor to Italy and where they found adjoining rooms in the Hôtel des Saints-Pères, Mabel's resistance collapsed. "In one night I threw it all away and nothing counted for me but Reed." For his part, Reed had known many girls since he had broken off his engagement to Madeleine Filon but his relationships with them had been of a fleeting nature. In Mabel he discovered not a girl but a mature woman and one, moreover, who not only attracted him physically but with whom he felt a strong intellectual affinity. Yet for all the sincerity and depth of his love for Mabel, Reed was not the sort of man who could cut himself off from the outside world and the fascination it would ever hold for him. He could not say of love, as did Mabel, that nothing else "counted for me." He could not live, as Mabel's fierce possessiveness required, on an emotional island-for-two. Almost immediately this difference in their personalities, which would lead in the future to a series of passionate battles and equally passionate reconciliations, made itself apparent. As Mabel wrote in *Movers and Shakers:*

> *The second morning in Paris a prodigious knocking on Reed's door made him leap away from me to go to his room, and I heard a hearty voice accosting him:*
>
> *"Hey, you scoundrel—don't you know the sun is overhead? ... I heard you were in Paris—get thee pants, old son, and come for déjeuner..." It was Waldo Peirce, and Reed closed the door between our rooms and I heard the two male voices, insouciant and gay, chaffing each other. He dressed quickly and went out, and my heart began to break a little right then.*

Mabel's heart broke "a little" more than once during the next months she and Reed spent at her lovely Villa Curonia in Italy. Though she possessed his attention totally at times, there were times when it would slip away from her. In the beginning she lost it to the beauty of cathedrals and frescoes whose magnificence was a fresh discovery for Reed. Then she lost it to the lively company of people she herself had invited to her villa—writers and musicians like Carl Van Vechten, Gertrude Stein, Arthur Rubinstein. And finally she lost it to Reed's own conscience.

As the weeks drifted by, during which he passed his days in visits to monuments or in lazy swims in a nearby pool, he began to grow restless and to feel the need of purposeful activity. It was all very well to admire what men had achieved in past centuries, but what of the achievements, as yet unfulfilled, of his own? And, especially, what of his part in them? He received news from home that the Paterson strike had failed, with the silkworkers returning poorer than ever to their looms. The final audit of the pageant, moreover, proved that they had lost instead of made money for the strikers with their inspirational yet costly production. Reed grew gloomy and dismal. The very monuments and new friends so enchanting to him upon his arrival be- came, like his indolent existence, ever more mean- ingless until—as if bitterly berating himself—he wrote:

Here where the olden poets came in beauty to die
I sit in a walled high garden, far from the sound of
   change,

Watching the great clouds boil up from the Vallom-
  brosa range
And sunlight pour through the black cypresses,
  drenching the vineyard dry.
Here is the drunken peace of the sensuous sick—
  and here am I. . . .

The poem ended in a plea to the woman who had
enclosed him in her "walled high garden":

O let us shake off this smothering silky death, let us
  go away,
My dearest old dear
Mabel! What are we living things doing here?

Mabel responded to his appeal and in mid-
September they sailed back to New York, where
Reed moved into the beautiful white rooms at
23 Fifth Avenue. The two lovers soon began to
quarrel, however. Mabel could not help wanting to
keep all of Reed for herself and was jealous of anyone else, or anything else—even the daily newspaper. As she wrote in *Movers and Shakers:*

> *What the morning paper said was happening*
> *in Mexico, or in Russia or at the Poles, seemed*
> *to make Reed's heart beat faster than I could,*
> *and I didn't like that. I felt doomed.*
>
> *"Listen to this—" he would cry and then*
> *he'd read the thing out loud, crackling the*
> *sheets of grayish paper, getting the still-damp*
> *print on his fingers, using me merely as a focus,*
> *to intensify the loss I felt of his attention.*

Mabel's persistent possessiveness drove Reed to break with her once and to leave her the following message:

Goodbye, my darling. I cannot live with you. You smother me. You crush me. You want to kill my spirit. I love you better than life but I do not want to die in my spirit. I am going away to save myself....

Mabel was bereft, while Reed, as she later wrote:

... wandered without knowing where he was going until he found himself stumbling up to Copey's door in Cambridge. Dear old Copey, who had told him he would never be a writer till he'd been a lover. He went up to Copey wild-eyed and disheveled.

"I've been a lover," he shouted, "but now I've lost my love! Tell me what to do! I can't stand it!"

"You go and tie your head up in a Turkish towel soaked in cold water," Copey told him, "and then come back and tell me about it."

Instead Reed returned to Mabel and there was a reconciliation. He had been as unable as she to bear the separation.

But even after that, Reed was not at home as often as Mabel would have liked. He was forever running off to her rival—the outside world. He found work as managing editor of the *Masses*. He became involved in helping out a friend under indictment for his participation in the Paterson strike. Wandering about his old Village haunts, he found material for new poems, new stories. . . .

Yet whatever he did, it never seemed enough to him. Where was the fame and glory he had dreamed of when he had felt the best of both worlds almost within his grasp? Though his contact with the *Metropolitan* had been promising, nothing had come of it. In addition, he felt hemmed in by everyday life and the boy from Oregon in him yearned for the excitement of a new frontier. Soon, however, that yearning was satisfied and in a way that surpassed all Reed's expectations.

seven:

In the spring of 1913 a peasant rebellion had broken out in Mexico and by the fall of the same year it had taken on the proportions of a violent civil war. The *Metropolitan* was looking for a special correspondent to send to Mexico, and Lincoln Steffens suggested Reed. Carl Hovey decided to take a chance on the young reporter whose work had already impressed him. An editorial conference was held in a secluded corner of the bar of the old Holland House in New York, with Reed, Steffens, Hovey, and two other representatives of the magazine: Finley Peter Dunne, the writer and humorist, and H. J. Whigham, an Englishman who was president and secretary of the *Metropolitan*. Reed presented his requirements—a camera and an ample expense account. But the question then arose as to which part of the fighting front he should cover, for the war in Mexico was a complicated affair.

On one side stood a military dictatorship, run by

the arbitrary will of a ruthless man—a drunkard and a cocaine addict—General Victoriano Huerta. His troops went by the name of Federals though most Mexicans called them *Huertistas*. Huerta represented the arrogance and terror that had ruled Mexico for centuries, ever since the Spaniards had first conquered its proud, peaceful people. He owed his support to the fabulously wealthy landowners for whom the Mexican peons had worked in a state of semiserfdom, generation after generation. Before the civil war, one family alone had owned seventeen million acres of land.

On the other side stood the Mexican peasantry— the peons. In the southern state of Morelos, they were fighting under Emiliano Zapata, a peasant revolutionary leader. In the north they had banded together into the Constitutionalist armies under the provisional government of Venustiano Carranza, who had established himself as First Chief of the Revolution. Though initially Carranza had participated in the fighting, he was a man of thought rather than action and had withdrawn to western Mexico, far from the battlefront, where he watched over the progress of his generals on the field.

One of those generals was a former bandit called Pancho Villa. In March of 1913, Villa had raised a peasant guerrilla force and with them had defeated the Federals in northern Mexico at Jiménez, captured Chihuahua City and descended in a lightning

91

raid on Juárez. He had set up a wing of the rebel government in the north where he was distributing confiscated land to the peons and giving money and food to the poor. A kind of Mexican Robin Hood, he had risen from relative obscurity in the space of a few short months to become a beloved savior of his people.

After some discussion around the table at the Holland House, it was decided that Reed should cover the Mexican war from Villa's camp. To add further prestige to his credentials as a journalist, it was considered advisable for him to obtain an assignment from a large daily newspaper as well. He secured one from the *New York World*, and a few days later he took a train to Texas.

In his hotel in El Paso, he found the lobby crowded with people—rich Mexican landowners who had fled with fortunes in gold sewn into their saddle blankets; Wall Street men nervous over their Mexican holdings; detectives, secret agents, journalists. The journalists were trying to pick up news of the Mexican war from refugees or recent arrivals, but Reed was after the kind of on-the-spot reporting he had done in Paterson and he left El Paso for Presidio, Texas, on the American side of the Rio Grande.

On the opposite bank of the river lay the Mexican town of Ojinaga, which was held by Federal forces under General Mercado. It was not Reed's job to deal with the Federals, but he was seeking a pretext for entering the country, and he sent a messenger with a note to Mercado requesting an interview. The reply came not from General Mercado but from still another Federal general, Pascual Orozco, who had intercepted Reed's note:

Esteemed and Honored Sir: If you set foot inside of Ojinaga, I will stand you sideways against a wall, and with my own hand take great pleasure in shooting furrows in your back.

It was one thing, Reed discovered, to discuss a war assignment in the comfortable security of the Holland House. It was quite another to contemplate it, as he did now, wading through the shallow yellow waters of the Rio Grande toward the opposite shore. "When I first crossed the border deadliest fear gripped me," he wrote in *Almost Thirty*. "I was afraid of death, of mutilation, of a strange land and strange people whose speech and thought I did not know. But a terrible curiosity urged me on. . . ."

In Ojinaga, Reed picked his way past dozing sentries through the rubble of white, dusty streets. The town had been lost and retaken five times by the *Huertistas*. The roofless houses were gutted by cannon shot. An ancient church stood windowless among the bare ruined dwellings. In empty doorways women and children stooped over small fires boiling corncobs and dried meat.

Reed found General Mercado "a fat, pathetic,

Pancho Villa

worried, undecided little man, who blubbered and
blustered a long tale about how the United States
army had come across the river and helped Villa to
win the battle of Tierra Blanca." It was a lie, of
course. The Americans had not crossed the border.

But Reed knew that the general had to lie. How else could he explain why the well-equipped, well-trained army of the dictatorship had been put to rout time and again by a shaggy band of poorly armed, illiterate peasants led by a onetime bandit?

Reed stole away from Ojinaga before General Orozco could discover his presence and went toward Chihuahua where that onetime bandit Pancho Villa had his headquarters. There on the Plaza de Armas thousands of people had massed before the palace to witness a ceremony in which Villa was to be awarded a medal. Reed later described the scene to his American readers:

"Ya viene!" "Here he comes!" "Viva Villa!" "Villa, the Friend of the Poor!"

The roar began at the back of the crowd and swept like fire in heavy growing crescendo until it seemed to toss thousands of hats above their heads. The band in the courtyard struck up the Mexican national air, and Villa came walking down the street.

He was dressed in an old plain khaki uniform, with several buttons lacking. He hadn't recently shaved, wore no hat, and his hair had not been brushed. He walked a little pigeon-toed, humped over, with his hands in his trouser pockets. As he entered the aisle between the rigid lines of soldiers he seemed slightly embarrassed, and grinned and nodded

to a compadre *here and there in the ranks. At*
the foot of the grand staircase, Governor Chao
and Secretary of State Terrazzas joined him in
full-dress uniform . . . and all the brilliant crowd
of officers in the room saluted stiffly.

It was Napoleonic!

Villa hesitated for a minute, pulling his mus-
tache and looking very uncomfortable, finally
gravitated toward the throne, which he tested
by shaking the arms, and then sat down.

The officers began to make long, flowery speeches
in the formal Mexican tradition. They lauded Villa
for his personal bravery, his invincible courage, his
inspiring patriotism. . . . Through it all Villa listened, occasionally yawning, amused and at the
same time bored by the high-flown oratory. Finally,
with an impressive gesture, a colonel stepped forward with the small pasteboard box which held the
medal.

An expectant hush fell upon everyone, even
the crowd in the square. Villa looked at the
medal, scratching his head, and, in a reverent
silence, said clearly: "This is a hell of a little
thing to give a man for all that heroism you are
talking about!" And the bubble of Empire was
pricked then and there with a great shout of
laughter.

They waited for him to speak—to make a
conventional address of acceptance. But as he

*looked around the room at those brilliant, edu-
cated men, who said that they would die for
Villa, the peon, and meant it, and as he caught
sight through the door of the ragged soldiers,
who had forgotten their rigidity and were
crowding eagerly into the corridor with eyes
fixed eagerly on the* compañero *that they
loved, he realized something of what the Revolution signified.*

*Puckering up his face, as he did always when
he concentrated intensely, he leaned across the
table in front of him and poured out, in a voice
so low that people could hardly hear: "There is
no word to speak. All I can say is my heart is
all to you." Then he nudged Chao and sat
down, spitting violently on the floor; and Chao
pronounced the classic discourse.*

When reporting of this kind began to reach the
United States, the editor of the *Metropolitan* knew
he had made the right choice in sending the twenty-
six-year-old John Reed to Mexico. Here was no dry
analyst of events, but a writer of bold descriptive
gifts. Reed did not merely tell his readers what he
observed, he created a vivid reportage filled with
rich images through which they could see what
was happening as if they themselves were present.
Until Reed's dispatches began to appear, Villa had
seemed a bloodthirsty bandit to the American people, a caricature of all that was ruthless, naive,
primitive, and nothing more. In Reed's writing

the State, or seemed
to. Terrazas was as
subservient as Ben-
avides.

V's actions and move-
ments were like those
of a wild animal. When
he stood up, he was
awkward and stiffish
below the knees, from
much horse-back riding.
: Above the waist, with hands
and arms and trunk he
would with the marvelous
- swiftness and sureness of
a ~~stiff~~ coyote. His mouth
hung open, and when
it did not smile, his
face looked good-natured,
almost simple. His
eyes, dark, perfectly
round, blood-shot,
shallow, were really
the desperate things
about him. Absolutely
hot and steely. Did not
say much. Spoke very
little and then
stutters, by ill. Wear-
ing business suit brown
shoes, felt hat. Has
never been in uniform

Pages from Reed's Mexican notebooks

98

the street stood an
ancient Spanish
church, and beside
that was the white
bare wall of the
Hacienda itself, while
beyond it great palms
towered up from the
patio, whence came
the sound of a fountain.

Plaza
Church   Hacienda
Palms
Square
Square
Houses both sides
Road
White
church
with own
and green
violet studded
doors

99

about Villa that caricature became rounded out skillfully into a portrayal of the real man. This is what the *Metropolitan* wanted for its public, and Carl Hovey wired Reed: YOU ARE SENDING US GREAT STUFF. WE ARE ABSOLUTELY DELIGHTED WITH YOUR WORK...

While Reed was in Chihuahua, he often went to see the guerrilla chief. Their meetings took place either in Villa's house or in the busy office, crowded with his rough and devoted *compañeros,* where Villa attended to the administrative details of his job as Governor of the State of Chihuahua and General of the Northern Division of the Constitutionalist armies. Though Villa was noted for his refusal to receive journalists, he never refused to see Reed. It was not only that he was won over by the young reporter's attractive personality or even by the gifts Reed had brought him—a saddle and a rifle with a gold nameplate on it as well as a Maxim silencer. The ex-bandit was intrigued by the sort of questions Reed posed and which no one had ever put to him before. What did he think of votes for women? What was his opinion of socialism?

"Socialism—is it a thing?" Villa answered. "I only see it in books, and I do not read much." And on the subject of woman's rights, Reed described Villa's reaction in the following scene:

Once I asked him if women would vote in the

new Republic. He was sprawled out on his bed; with his coat unbuttoned. "Why, I don't think so," he said, startled, suddenly sitting up. "What do you mean—vote? Do you mean elect a government and make laws?" I said I did and that women already were doing it in the United States. "Well," he said, scratching his head: "if they do it up there I don't see that they shouldn't do it down here." The idea seemed to amuse him enormously. He rolled it over and over in his mind, looking at me and away again. "It may be as you say," he said; "but I have never thought about it. Women seem to me to be things to protect, to love. They have no sternness of mind. They can't consider anything for its right or wrong. They are full of pity and softness. Why," he said, "a woman would not give an order to execute a traitor."

"I am not so sure of that, mi General," I said. "Women can be crueller and harder than men."

He stared at me, pulling his mustache. And then he began to grin. He looked slowly to where his wife was setting the table for lunch. "Oiga," he said, "come here. Listen. Last night I caught three traitors crossing the river to blow up the railroad. What shall I do with them? Shall I shoot them or not?"

Embarrassed, she seized his hand and kissed it. "Oh, I don't know anything about that," she said. "You know best."

101

"No," said Villa. "I leave it entirely to you. Those men were going to try to cut our communication between Juárez and Chihuahua. They were traitors—Federals. What shall I do? Shall I shoot them or not?"

"Oh, well, shoot them," said Mrs. Villa.

Villa chuckled delightedly. "There is something in what you say," he remarked, and for days afterward went around asking the cook and the chambermaids whom they would like to have for President of Mexico.

While Americans were being fascinated by Reed's reports, Villa himself found it somewhat comical that a rich magazine in the United States was willing to pay a man like Reed good money to find out what *he* thought. But then that was their affair; his was war—and war, not for the sake of war, but, as Reed discovered, for the sake of a new kind of Mexico in which the peon would own the land he worked and in which his children could go to school and learn to read. Land and education for the people—that was Pancho Villa's goal. Beyond that he had no personal ambitions, for he regarded Carranza as his *jefe*—his chief. Though they would later have bitter differences, at the time he saw the educated Carranza, not himself, as the future President of Mexico.

Villa was preparing to launch a major attack from the north on the main citadel of the enemy, the city of Torreón, but nobody knew when he would decide to move. Meanwhile, Reed did not want to remain on the edge of the war and to write his stories about it from a distance or from hearsay. He wanted to live among the ordinary peons who were doing the fighting. One morning he heard that, in the upland plain of Durango, the armies of General Urbina—another rebel officer—were approaching the fighting front from a point farther south and he made up his mind to go to Durango.

It was a risky decision. The countryside was infested with *colorados*—Huerta volunteers, who were crueler and fiercer than the Federal regulars. They could easily cut a man to pieces before he could reach in his pocket for the credentials which vouched for his neutrality as a war correspondent and which few of them would be able to read anyway. In addition, the railroad line was laid with dynamite as far as Jiménez and after that there was no rail at all, just empty prairie and mountain. There were no horses to be had, for every available mount was needed by the fighting men.

Reed nevertheless set off for Durango—first in a bullet-ridden troop train, then in the two-wheeled gig of a peddler. He spent his days driving over hard dusty roads. He passed his nights around low campfires in dark gullies or on the edge of some deserted hacienda. He went through the towns of Jiménez, San Pedro, San Isidro, Magistral, until finally he reached Las Nieves, where the peddler dropped him off and turned swiftly back, for beyond Las Nieves was the front.

At a nearby hacienda, Reed found General Urbina and his soldiers, who were a picturesque and ragged lot. Some wore overalls, others the *charro* jackets of peons, still others tight *vaquero* trousers. A few had shoes, most of them only cowhide sandals and the rest were barefoot. This peasant band was the famed *La Tropa* which had already distinguished itself in battle on behalf of the Mexican Revolution. In a few days they were going to depart for the front, and Reed gained permission from General Urbina to accompany *La Tropa* on the march.

He rode along in an old coach loaded with cases of dynamite across the savage prairie where "black shiny chaparral, the height of a mule's back, scraped the side of the coach; Spanish bayonet and the great barrel-cactus watched us like sentinels from the skyline of the desert. And always the mighty Mexican vultures circled over us, as if they knew we were going to war."

Up ahead, the red-white-and-green flag of Mexico fluttering in its lead, *La Tropa* was strung out for half a mile—"rifles slung at their saddles, four or five cartridge-belts crossed over their chests, high, flapping sombreros, immense spurs chiming as they rode, bright-colored serapes strapped on behind."

In the beginning the men of *La Tropa* were sus-

104

picious of Reed. He was an American—a gringo—
and to them all gringos were enemies. The only
Americans they had ever met were those who
owned the mines in Mexico and who had forced
the peons to work like slaves. They could not
believe that Reed was genuinely interested in them
or sympathetic to their cause, as his questions appeared to indicate. Though they were outwardly
friendly, laughing without malice at his halting
Spanish and calling him in a kidding way
"Meester," more than one of them was convinced
he had been sent by the foreigners, or perhaps even
by the *Huertistas*, to spy on their movements.

Reed was aware of this and sought to break
down the barrier which separated him from these
men. There was no Bill Haywood here in the Mexican desert, however, as there had been in the Paterson jail, to tell the others he was trustworthy. He
had to win the Mexicans' confidence on his own,
and they soon saw he was no pampered American.
When they challenged him to drink half a bottle of
sotol—a liquor whose potency was celebrated—he
drank it down in one go. When they dared him to
perform the *jota* during the dances held at night in
deserted haciendas along the way, he stumbled and
struggled until at last he mastered the swift turns.
When they slaughtered a steer and had no time to
cook the meat, he wasn't too squeamish to join
them in tearing at the raw carcass. And when the
choice lay before him to live with the officers or to

sleep in the hot, crowded *cuartels*, the quarters of
the men, Reed chose the *cuartels*.

One night, however, a trooper called Julian
Reyes, who still guarded his suspicions of the gringo
reporter, sat down next to Reed.

He was far gone in sotol—*his eyes burned
like a fanatic's.*

He turned on me suddenly:

"Are you going to fight with us?"

*"No," I said. "I am a correspondent. I am
forbidden to fight."*

*"It is a lie," he cried. "You don't fight be-
cause you are afraid to fight. In the face of God
our Cause is Just."*

*"Yes, I know that. But my orders are not to
fight."*

*"What do I care for orders. . . ? We want no
correspondents. We want rifles and killing. . . .
Coward!* Huertista! *. ."*

*"That's enough," cried someone, and I looked
up to see Longinos Güereca standing over me.
"Julian Reyes, you know nothing. This* compañero *comes thousands of miles by the sea
and the land to tell his countrymen the truth
of the fight for Liberty. He goes into battle
without arms, he's braver than you are, because you have a rifle. Get out now, and don't
bother him any more!"*

The last fragment of resistance to Reed dissolved and the men took him in as one of their own, a *compadre*. Around the campfires at night, the soldiers told him about the hardness and poverty of their lives and about their hopes for a new democratic Mexico. They shared their jokes and songs with him, and often one of them would lend Reed his horse. Then he would ride along with *La Tropa*, talking to the men. They were a rough band of ex-outlaws and some were so poor they did not even own a serape, yet their honesty made a deep impression on Reed. He had a hundred and fifty pesos, which he put conspicuously beside him when he slept. It was never touched. Though food and tobacco were scarce, the *compañeros* saw to it that Reed was always well supplied. He discovered both pride and generosity in the ex-outlaws too, for whenever he tried to pay for anything, they considered it an insult.

Reed had the opportunity to witness the already legendary bravery of *La Tropa* when a band of a thousand *colorados*—the ruthless Huerta volunteers—swept down one morning on the outpost at La Cadena in a surprise attack. Reed had remained behind with a hundred troopers who had been left to guard the mountain pass at La Cadena while the main body of *La Tropa* had moved on ahead. These hundred, however, did not hesitate to meet the advancing horde in a fierce counterattack. They took to horse and even those who had no arms rode forward with the shout, "Let's go out and strangle them with our bare hands." In the bloody battle that followed, nearly all the troopers were slaughtered, and Reed himself was forced to flee.

"I wasn't very frightened," he wrote later. "It just seemed to me that if I didn't get away I wouldn't be doing my job well. I kept thinking to myself: 'Well, this is certainly an experience. I'm going to have something to write about.'"

He very nearly didn't, however, for the desert was a flat tableland from which he could be seen for miles around as he ran toward the hills—throwing off his camera, then his overcoat—until finally he stumbled over a mesquite root into a small arroyo. There he hid while a band of *colorados*, not ten feet from where he lay, rode past him, shooting at the last survivors of the little garrison.

Later, after tramping a hundred miles alone across the desert, Reed caught up with the main body of *La Tropa* and rejoined them on the march. From time to time he left the fighting front to go on special assignments. He interviewed the First Chief of the Revolution, still in solitude, Venustiano Carranza. On another occasion he covered the case of a multimillionaire Scotch landowner purported to have been shot by Villa's men and whose death caused a scandal that almost, but not quite, brought about foreign intervention. But he always returned to the fighting and during the long drive on Torreón—the main fortress of the Huerta army—he rode in the troop train with Villa's men. There he had the opportunity to observe the close unity between the peasant leader and his peon soldiers. "When a ragged mob of fierce brown men with hand bombs and rifles rush the bullet-swept streets of an ambushed town," he wrote, "Villa is among them, like any common soldier."

Many battles raged around Torreón until the city tottered under Villa's blows. During the last days of the attack, censorship was imposed and Reed was unable to send out his dispatches. He realized, too, that after the fall of Torreón, the nature of the war would change from wild guerrilla fighting to a confrontation of orderly armies in formation and thus would be of less interest to him. Moreover, he had become sickened by the sight of slaughter. He decided to leave Mexico and, stealing away in a gasoline car on the railroad line, he crossed back over the frontier and returned to El Paso.

He had spent four months covering the Mexican War and the experience changed him in many ways. It gave him firm confidence in himself as a man and as a writer. "I wrote better than I have ever written," he later commented in *Almost Thirty*. In the same work, he spoke of the deadly fear that had gripped him when he had first crossed the border, yet afterwards "I discovered that bullets are not very terrifying, that the fear of death is not such a great thing." But more important, perhaps, was his growing personal identification with the common people and their lives, which had become reinforced and clarified:

> *That four months of riding hundreds of miles across the blazing plains, sleeping on the ground with the* hombres ... *being with them intimately in play, in battle, was perhaps the most satisfactory period of my life. I made good with these wild fighting men, and with myself. I loved them and I loved the life. I found myself again.*

Many of his friends had sent appreciative letters to Reed while he was still in Mexico about the stories which had already begun to appear under his by-line in the *Metropolitan* and the *World*. Walter Lippmann had written:

> *It's kind of embarrassing to tell a fellow you know that he's a genius, but you're in a wild country now. I can't begin to tell you how good the articles are. . . . You have perfect eyes, and your power of telling leaves nothing to be desired. . . . If all history had been reported as you are doing this, Lord! I say that with Jack Reed reporting begins. Incidentally, of course, the stories are literature.*

Still, Reed had not been aware of the extent of his fame back home. When he returned to New York, however, he saw a large ad in *The New York*

110

Times announcing his *Metropolitan* articles with a drawing depicting him as a heroic figure. He saw delivery trucks of the *World* carrying his name on their sides and proclaiming him "America's Kipling." He learned that the great Kipling himself had said of John Reed: "His articles in the *Metropolitan* made me *see* Mexico." In celebrating the deeds of his *compañeros* in Mexico, Reed himself had become a celebrity.

eight:

In July of 1914 D. Appleton and Company published *Insurgent Mexico*, a book that Reed based on the articles he had written for the *Metropolitan* and the *World*. It was praised by friends and public alike, but the man whose good opinion of it meant perhaps more to Reed than anyone else's was the professor at Hollis Hall to whom he dedicated the volume. Copeland wrote his former student that *Insurgent Mexico* was not only "all good and more than good," but that its author was a "born writer" —a fact, the professor added dryly, which he had discovered long ago.

Upon his return from Mexico there was hardly a magazine or newspaper that was not clamoring for Reed's services and, in addition, willing to pay the highest prices for them. Carl Hovey sought to obtain the exclusive rights to his work for the *Metropolitan*. Reed decided to remain a free-lancer, however, for he was enjoying the sudden luxury of choice.

In the white rooms at 23 Fifth Avenue, he and Mabel picked up their life together. Neither one was in a quarreling mood at the moment, and he became the star of her salon with a "Reed in Mexico" evening. But he was impatient to get back to work. He needed money and not only for himself now. It had not been uncommon for Hovey to receive cables from Mexico which included such messages as: "When there is that much to my credit please send five hundred to Mrs. C. J. Reed Wickersham Apartments Portland Oregon." Reed was at last able to contribute to his mother's support and henceforth would always transfer to her a good part of whatever money he earned.

Almost before Mabel had a chance to become used to his presence again, he left New York to hasten off to Ludlow, Colorado, and a new assignment. There had been a massacre of striking miners and their families in Ludlow on the morning of April 20, 1914. Thirty-three people, more than half of them women and children, had been either machine-gunned or burned to death by a state militia made up of recently sworn-in ex-policemen and gunmen. The country was shocked by the massacre, and Reed was sent to investigate on behalf of the *Metropolitan*.

When he arrived on the scene, he found "stoves, pots and pans still half full of food that had been cooking that terrible morning, baby carriages, piles of half-burned clothes, children's toys all riddled with bullets, the scorched mouths of the tent cellars . . . all that remained of the entire worldly possessions of 1,200 people." He saw the "death hole" from which the charred bodies had been unearthed. This was the first time he had come in contact with industrial violence of such scope and he set out to find out how and why it had taken place.

The coal miners had been striking for demands that included an eight-hour day, recognition of their union, and safety conditions in mines that had the highest death rate from accidents in the nation. Many of these demands were guaranteed by the laws of the state of Colorado, Reed discovered, but the laws had never been enforced because the powerful coal companies, dominated by Rockefeller interests, controlled the state government through politicians they had placed in office. When the strikers sought negotiations, they were answered with force. They were driven from their houses and obliged to live in tent colonies. Then the state militia was ordered to machine-gun and burn the tents.

But what marked the Ludlow strike as exceptional in the labor struggles of this period, Reed found, was not the violence wrought by the coal owners but the fact that after the massacre the strikers themselves took up arms. They organized military companies. They established positions on

After the massacre of many of their families, the striking mineworkers in Ludlow, Colorado, took up arms. This photo illustrated Reed's article "The Colorado War," which appeared in the Metropolitan *in July 1914.*

the surrounding hills. More battles occurred as mine shafts were attacked and burned, and more strikers were killed. At last President Wilson ordered out federal troops to disarm both sides, and the conflict ended . . . in victory for John D. Rockefeller, Jr. The union was not recognized; its demands were ignored.

The Ludlow massacre was a corroboration to Reed of what he had learned in the Paterson jail

115

about class war. "I have seen and reported many strikes," he wrote later in *Almost Thirty*, "most of them desperate struggles for the bare necessities of life; and all I have witnessed only confirms my first idea of the class-struggle and its inevitability." His highly documented investigation of the Ludlow strike was called "The Colorado War." When it appeared in the July issue of the *Metropolitan*, Reed's editor praised it unconditionally. He did not seem to mind that a bookstore in Denver canceled its standing order for the *Metropolitan* because of the "vile unwarranted sensational lies" it claimed the piece contained. To Hovey this reaction was merely one more proof of the effectiveness of Reed's reportage.

In the spring of 1914 Reed accompanied Mabel to Provincetown where they lived for a few weeks in a rented cottage by the sea. But soon another issue drove him to leave her side temporarily. An anti-American provocation on the part of General Huerta had resulted in a partial American intervention in the Mexican War. President Wilson ordered the marines to occupy Veracruz and mobilized other forces on the border. Reed foresaw a danger that the expeditionary force, bent initially on pacification, would turn into a conquering army that would overrun Mexico and, while destroying the Huerta forces, would destroy the revolutionary forces as well. To prevent this if he could, he went down to Washington where he was received by

Secretary of State William Jennings Bryan and by the President himself. Woodrow Wilson assured Reed that America had no imperialist designs on Mexico, but as the President's secretary explained: "The President opened his mind to you completely, with the understanding that you were not to quote him." Reed was unable to see the interview into print.

By now, however, the *Metropolitan* had other plans for him. Europe was on the brink of war, and Hovey wired Reed, alerting him to be ready to go abroad as the magazine's correspondent. Reed left Provincetown to pay a quick visit to his mother in Portland, while Mabel sailed for her villa in Italy. In Portland, Reed found himself a hometown celebrity, invited to teas, luncheons, and dinners everywhere. He had not seen his mother in two years, and she was relieved and delighted to have him safely home from Mexico. But being the mother of a war correspondent was not an easy role. It was with fresh worry that Margaret Reed saw her son depart a few days later, in the fastest continental train he could find, for New York and then for a new battlefront.

The First World War grew out of the rivalry between European nations for control of markets, sources of raw materials, territory, trade routes, and colonies. In the conflict two great alliances faced each other. On one side stood France, Russia, England, with Italy and Japan joining them even-

117

tually as allies. On the other side stood Germany and Austria with their eventual allies, Turkey and Bulgaria. The first shots were fired in the early summer of 1914 when the Austrian armies, backed by the Germans who claimed they were seeking a "place in the sun" as a nation, moved into Serbia. By the end of the summer all of Europe, with the exception of Scandinavia, Holland, Spain, Portugal and Switzerland, had been drawn into the war.

The immediate official reaction in America was expressed by President Wilson's declaration: "The United States must be neutral in fact as well as in name during these days which are to try men's souls." Former President Theodore Roosevelt—who had appointed C. J. Reed United States marshal and who soon would be working beside C.J.'s son on the contributing staff of the *Metropolitan*—advised the American people against "taking sides one way or the other" in the "bitter and vindictive hatreds" of Europe.

At the same time an initially small but rapidly growing anti-German sentiment made itself felt in the country, along with pressure to involve America in the conflict. Newspapers began to be filled with inflammatory propaganda containing accounts of German atrocities. Reed wrote an article in the *Masses* called "The Traders' War" in which he described the "editorial chorus in America which pretends to believe—would have us believe—that the White and Spotless Knight of Modern Democ-

118

racy is marching against the Unspeakably Vile Monster of Medieval Militarism." He did not believe that the Allies were fighting, as Wilson would say later, to make the world "safe for democracy," nor that an Allied victory could possibly make it so. He analyzed the nature of this First World War in a way in which most historians would come to look back on it decades later, after the rise of Fascism in Germany and Italy and the subsequent outbreak of World War II. "The real war," Reed wrote in his *Masses* article, "of which this sudden outburst of death and destruction is only an incident, began long ago. It has been raging for tens of years, but its battles have been so little advertised that they have been hardly noted. It is a clash of traders." But this seemed a radical viewpoint to many at the time and public opinion was far from unanimously in agreement with Reed when he added, "We must not be duped by this editorial buncombe about Liberalism going forth to Holy War against Tyranny. This is not Our War."

The common interests of the oppressed working people of Europe bound them by stronger ties to each other, he believed, than to the governments that sought to turn them into soldiers. He felt sympathy for the men, whatever their country, who would die in the vast and brutal slaughter that seemed imminent. Yet he was determined to do his job well and on the Italian steamship which carried him across the ocean "under cover of darkness, with

119

lights hidden," he began to make notes for his first article.

Reed landed at Naples, then moved up to Rome. He had been asked by the *Metropolitan* to cover Italy's entry into the war on the side of the Germans and Austrians. The Italian government was slow in making a decision, however, and in the uncertain atmosphere of rumor and speculation which might last for many weeks, Reed found nothing newsworthy to report. Meanwhile, he heard that the German armies in France were advancing and he decided to make his way northward. He traveled to Geneva in neutral Switzerland, and from there he took the last train for Paris.

The City of Light with its bright cafés and crowded boulevards, which Reed had known during his first trip abroad, had been vastly altered by the war. The café terraces were empty, the storefronts were shuttered, the streets deserted. At night the only light came from arcs which intermittently swept the sky in search of German planes; the only sound was that of troops marching along the cobblestones.

But though Reed felt the proximity of the war, he and the other journalists in Paris were totally isolated from it. The news was scant. There were only censored official announcements. Moreover, no rights or status whatsoever were accorded war correspondents in World War I. On the contrary, "with every army the correspondent is as popular as a floating mine," angrily wrote one of their number, the noted Richard Harding Davis, who had years of war reporting behind him. The journalists were aware that Paris was frantically preparing for a siege, that the Germans were but a few miles away, yet not one of them, no matter how brilliant his credentials, was allowed to join the forces in battle.

It seemed to Reed that the only way to break out of this enforced isolation was to break the law. Robert Dunn of the New York *Post* agreed with him. Pretending illness, Reed and Dunn secured a pass for Nice on the Mediterranean coast where, so they told the authorities, they wanted to go to recover their health, and they started south in a rented car. The pass carried them through the defenses of Paris and as soon as they had left the city behind, they turned east and north.

Passing swarms of refugees on the roadsides, they drove through villages that lay in smoldering ruins. They spent a night near an ammunition dump, talking to the soldiers on guard, and the next day they tried to reach the front. But no matter which road they took, they were always forced back and at last were caught by the British. The latter turned them over to the French gendarmerie, who sent them by slow stages to Tours, after making them sign a sworn statement that they would never venture near a battle zone again.

Though the experience had not been a total loss

and Reed had been able to complete an article for the *Metropolitan*, he had once again reached an impasse, for his movements in France were virtually blocked. He left Paris for London, hoping to unearth a story there, and from the English capital he sent back an article describing the mood of the country. He wrote of the indifference of British working people to a war that seemed to them remote from their problems. He contrasted this indifference with the zeal of the rich who, to his mind, were seeking to arouse a patriotic feeling in the workingman by displaying banners on their chauffeured Rolls-Royces proclaiming "Your King and Country Need You!" and by forming committees of society women who stood in front of the National Gallery handing out the white feathers of cowardice to men in civilian clothes. This article proved offensive to the president of the *Metropolitan*, H. J. Whigham, a Britisher himself, while Hovey considered it somewhat less than Reed's best, and the article was rejected.

Reed grew depressed and frustrated. His weeks in Europe were swiftly stretching into months. His work had proved disappointing, and he began to wonder whether he would ever be able to turn out really worthwhile impressions of the war. He knew what the *Metropolitan* expected of him—the kind of on-the-spot, human interest reporting he had done in the past. The magazine wanted the color and heroism and romance of Mexico. But in the European war Reed could discover neither romance nor heroics, only grim, mechanized annihilation. Moreover, he couldn't even get close enough to the men who were doing the fighting to write about them.

His frustration deepened when his personal affairs took a turn for the worse. Upon his arrival in Italy, Reed had found Mabel Dodge at her villa near Florence and she had traveled with him to Paris and to London. Mabel's feelings for Reed had begun to diminish, however. She wanted peace and emotional security and feared she would never be able to find either with him. She intuitively sensed the inevitability of a break between them, and this lessening in her affections came to her rescue to blunt the shock of final separation. Though their love appeared on the surface as binding as ever, when she left Europe now to go home, Reed was deeply disturbed by the subtle change in her attitude.

Back in Paris he discovered a married woman he had known in Greenwich Village. She was alone and ill and he took care of her. What began as the act of a good samaritan swiftly turned into a love affair. When Mabel heard of it in New York she was surprised to find how little she cared. The woman's husband took a different view, however. Returning suddenly from a trip, he threatened to shoot Reed on sight. But by that time Reed's own feelings for the girl had altered and he extricated himself from the marital tangle.

With characteristic candor, Reed made no attempt to hide what was happening to him either professionally or personally. In a letter to Hovey he wrote, "I have had terrible luck this trip. I haven't been afraid, and I don't want you to think so. But I just can't seem to make it so far. There are other reasons too quite distinct from the troubles I am now wearing out my heart on. I have really been through the deepest hell all around." He received a wire from New York suggesting he return for editorial consultations. But he was determined to prove himself and wrote back instead, asking for more money and more time. Hovey, whose basic confidence in Reed was unwavering, granted both, and Reed soon made the most of them.

He traveled in a roundabout way through neutral countries to Berlin where he sought the permission which had been denied him in France to visit the firing lines. It took several weeks to make arrangements, but the German authorities at last agreed to escort a visiting Senator from Indiana, Albert J. Beveridge, and a group of correspondents, among them Reed and Robert Dunn, across occupied France to the front in Belgium. They drove in German automobiles toward Lille and beyond, to Comines, Houthem. . . .

124

As the group approached the front they could hear the thunder of German batteries nearby, while German and French planes pursued each other overhead. They were taken to visit one of the quieter sectors. Even so, the constant bursting of shells in the vicinity made the majority of the group feel it had seen enough. Only Reed and Dunn wanted to press on to the trenches where soldiers were actually fighting. After supper at field headquarters, the two of them set off alone on foot with a German lieutenant as their guide. Reed described the experience in an article he wrote for the *Metropolitan* called "In the German Trenches."

We stumbled along the road in the pitch black night, Dunn and I and the officer.... The rain fell steadily. On our right the stumps of trees broken by shell fire pricked sharply up against the hellish illumination of the rockets. The whistle of bullets over our heads blended into an almost steady sound and lashed treetrunks like whips. Half a mile ahead on the left three big howitzers smote the air one after another with deep sound. Footsteps crunched the muddy road....

And now, suddenly, we were in the front trench. Leaning against its front wall men stood shoulder to shoulder, shielded by thin plates of steel, each pierced with a loophole through which the rifle lay. Sodden with the drenching rain, their bodies crushing into the oozy mud, they stood thigh-deep in thick brown water and shot eight hours of the twenty-four.... The shooters paid no attention to us. Through their loopholes they stared absorbed, alert, into the blackness, waiting until the next rocket should show the least movement....

Up a gentle hill straggled the French trench, a black gash pricked with rifle-flame. Between lay flat ooze, glistening like the slime of a sea-bed uncovered by an earthquake. Only a little way off lay the huddled, blue-coated bodies of the French in three thick, regular rows, just as they fell a week and a half ago, for there had been no cessation in the firing.

"Look," cried the lieutenant, "how they have been slowly sinking into the mud! Three days ago you could see more. See that hand, and that foot, sticking up out of the ground; the rest of the bodies have sunk."

We saw them, the hand stiff, five fingers spread wide like a drowning man's.

"No need of graves there. They are burying themselves!"

Throughout most of the night the two reporters remained in the trench with the soldiers. As it grew toward morning, one of the officers turned to them and, handing them a rifle, asked them if they would like to take a shot. Tense and on the edge of their

126

nerves, both of them pointed in the general direction of France and fired—then they left the dugout to return to the rear, following the men going off duty. As Reed wrote, in the conclusion to his article:

Along the road we caught up with the soldiers, straggling along with rifles carried under their arms, and drooping shoulders; silent, for the most part, with the silence of desperately weary men.... Suddenly a man immediately ahead began to scream. We could not see him in the dark, but we could hear moans and unintelligible yells, and the scuffling of struggling feet. A moment later the lieutenant flashed his pocket-lamp on and we saw him. A gag had been forced into his mouth; ropes bound his arms tightly to his sides; two comrades held him firmly by the elbows, forcing him forward. His wild, staring eyes snapped wide like a savage beast's at the sudden light—he wrenched his muddy shoulders convulsively to and fro. He was quite mad.

"Another one," muttered the lieutenant....

We walked briskly ahead, passing the last shuffling man, and were alone again, on the road to the farmhouse. None of us talked much —we had a good deal to think about.

Reed spent five months in Europe covering the war. When they were over, Carl Hovey was amply rewarded for his faith in the gifts of his correspondent. In the November and December issues of 1914 and in the March issue of 1915 appeared Reed's articles, "The Approach to War," "With the Allies," "German France"—interesting and informative pieces. But when his final story appeared in April 1915—announced by a banner sweeping the cover of the *Metropolitan:* JOHN REED's story of a NIGHT IN THE GERMAN TRENCHES—it marked an utterly new kind of writing about modern warfare and the men who participated in it. As Hovey wrote of this article in his reminiscences:

> *Upon his readers it had the effect of a revelation. For the first time the actual ordeal of the soldier—the endurance of mud, monotony, desperate fatigue, the nerve strain of apocalyptic lighting and earth-shaking guns ... all they had never known and scarcely guessed of the peculiar awfulness of the new kind of war—was flashed before them indelibly clear.*
>
> *The crushing indictment was the first of its kind. No longer was it possible for the stay-at-home who read it to dream of war as something clean and glorious, uplifting the sluggish spirit of man....*
>
> *And at last Reed himself had returned, wandering heart, obscure finances, genius and all; the writer sees him plainly to this day, stand-*

ing in the office doorway, a solid tower in his
bedraggled trench coat, holding out with a
modest smile his manuscript. He knew there
was no need to ask if he had done well.

The *Metropolitan* was eager to send Reed back
to France to do another series for the magazine.
Only one obstacle stood in the way—those random
shots he and Dunn had fired before leaving the
German lines. Dunn had mentioned them in one of
his dispatches in the *Post*, but though he had made
light of the incident, it took on a significance which
both surprised and irritated Reed and his fellow
reporter. Feeling in America had become more
sharply pro-Allied than ever, and editorials were
written denouncing the two men as pro-German.
Richard Harding Davis marched angrily into the
office of the *Metropolitan* and expressed his indig-
nation. Former President Theodore Roosevelt, who
by now had joined the *Metropolitan*'s staff, echoed
Davis's wrath. More importantly, the French authorities formally barred Reed and Dunn from
France.

To many the affair seemed to have been magni-
fied out of all reasonable proportion. Booth Tarkington, author of *Seventeen* and other popular
novels and short stories, wrote the *Metropolitan*
that Reed's and Dunn's gesture that night in the
trenches was merely "an intenser edition of taking
a glass of beer, as a sample, when being shown over

the brewery" and that "as far as they're concerned the thing should be forgotten." Yet in view of the French ban, something had to be done and it was clearly the influential Roosevelt who had to do it.

He telephoned the French ambassador in Washington and expressed the hope that an apology on Reed's part might induce the French to alter their decision. He followed up the phone call with letters. But, though Roosevelt tried genuinely to intervene on Reed's behalf, his own changed sentiments about the war—he was now strongly pro-Ally—won out in the end over his loyalty to his associate. The Colonel, as the former President was always called by his co-workers on the *Metropolitan*, asked Reed into his new office at the magazine and announced to him: "I have written to my friend Ambassador Jusserand to thank him for his consideration of your case, and to confess that my judgment is the same as his. Now I will read you my closing sentence: "If I were Marshal Joffre and Reed fell into my hands, I should have him court-martialed and shot.' "

Reed was furious but helpless. A return to France was out of the question. The *Metropolitan* was now considering sending him to Eastern Europe and, while plans were being made for the new assignment, he spent the next two months in New York. During that time he once again became a target for criticism. The *New Republic*, a magazine which had been recently founded and of which Walter Lippmann was one of the editors, published an article by Lippmann entitled "Legendary John Reed." In it Lippmann's criticisms of Reed were sharply personal but that sharpness came as no surprise to those who were aware of the growing divergence between the two men in their views on the conflict in Europe. Reed's general approach to politics, which included his slogan "This is not our war," seemed oversimplified to Lippmann. Reed in turn felt that the complicated editorial statements he found in the *New Republic*'s pages were nothing more than ideological preparations to justify America's eventual participation in the war. Deep-seated differences in opinion can affect personal judgments in subtle ways. Thus the man who less than a year before had been unconditional in his praise of Reed, labeling him a "genius" and calling his Mexican reportage "literature," now wrote:

> *I can't think of a form of disaster which John Reed hasn't tried and enjoyed. He has half-spilled himself into commercialism, had his head turned by flattery, tried to act like a cynical war-correspondent, posed as a figure out of Ibsen.... By temperament he is not a professional writer or reporter. He is a person who enjoys himself. Revolution, literature, poetry, they are only things which hold him at times, incidents merely of his living. Now and then he finds adventure by imagining it, oftener he*

transforms his own experience. He is one of those people who treat as serious possibilities such stock fantasies as shipping before the mast, rescuing women, hunting lions, or trying to fly around the world in an aeroplane. . . . Reed is one of the intractables, to whom the organized monotone and virtue of our civilization is unbearable. You would have to destroy him to make him fit. At times when he seemed to be rushing himself and others into trouble, when his ideas were especially befuddled, I have tried to argue with him. But all laborious elucidation he greets with pained boredom. . . . I don't know what to do about him. In common with a whole regiment of his friends, I have been brooding over his soul for years, and often I feel like saying to him what one of them said when Reed was explaining Utopia. "If I were establishing it, I'd hang you first, my dear Jack." But it would be a lonely Utopia.

It was criticism not unmingled with affection, yet Reed might well have resented the one-sidedness of the attack, for it was true that while he thoroughly enjoyed everything he did, at the same time his thinking was not flighty. When he said repeatedly in his articles these days, "This is not our war," he meant it, and he later proved just how much he meant it when, after America's entry into the conflict, he risked imprisonment for his anti-

132

war stand. He made no public counterattack on Lippmann, however. Perhaps he felt that Lippmann—no less a friend though somewhat less a radical than he formerly had been—was merely taking revenge for the lines Reed had once penned about him in his *Day in Bohemia:*

His face is almost placid,—but his eye,—
There is a vision born to prophecy!
He sits in silence, as one who has said:
"I waste not living words among the dead!"
Our all-unchallenged Chief! But were there one
Who builds a world, and leaves out all the fun,—
Who dreams a pageant, gorgeous, infinite,
And then leaves all the color out of it,—
Who wants to make the human race, and me,
March to a geometric Q.E.D.—
Who but must laugh, if such a man there be?
Who would not weep, if WALTER L. were he?

During his two months in New York, Reed wrote an article which dealt neither with labor strife nor with war but with an evangelist preacher, Billy Sunday. Along with George Bellows, who drew the illustrations for his article, "Back of Billy Sunday," which appeared in the *Metropolitan*, Reed went to Philadelphia where he sat in a tabernacle listening to Billy Sunday exhort the crowd to "come to Jesus" and to cease coveting material blessings but to look to the state of their souls. Reed was unable

133

to approach any subject without investigating the political implications behind it, and he sought out the businessmen who were backing the evangelist preacher through a Citizen's Committee which had secured pledges to the amount of $50,000. In his article Reed claimed that these men were using Billy Sunday as a tool to keep the poor in their place and to prevent them psychologically from demanding better living conditions. He quoted one of these men as saying, "Slums, you know, are largely the fault of those who live there—dirty, disreputable, vicious people." Reed treated the preacher himself without malice, but his satirical jibes at the men who indirectly profited from his philosophy were merciless.

During those two months in New York, too, Reed tried to pick up his relationship with Mabel, but she was determined now to break off their liaison. Though Reed urged her to believe that he loved her, despite his fleeting affair abroad, and that he sincerely wanted to marry her, she convinced him, as she wrote, "It's all finished with us." Reed was so overwrought that Lincoln Steffens felt compelled to intervene. He urged Mabel to take Reed back for the short time that remained before his departure for Eastern Europe. Mabel hesitated at first but "Steff made honesty seem petty, and compromise more large and generous than human sincerity." She agreed reluctantly . . . even agreed to a symbolic exchange of rings, and Reed left her side convinced that he and Mabel would be joined for life.

By March plans had materialized for the *Metropolitan* to send Reed back to Europe to cover the eastern sector of the war. Accompanying him on the assignment was Boardman Robinson, an artist who had worked on the staff of the *Tribune* and who was also an occasional contributor to the *Masses.* The *Metropolitan* gave Reed and Robinson an ample expense account and free reign in their choice of material. Soon colorful articles, along with Robinson's talented illustrations, were received in New York from Salonika, Belgrade, Sofia—and from obscure little cities with difficult names like Przemysl, Zaleszcyki, Prnjavor.

They were arrested time and again or handed expulsion orders, as they tried to enter restricted areas and reach the fighting fronts in the Balkans and in Russia. Yet more than once they managed to avoid sentries, board forbidden trains, cross blocked frontiers. On one occasion they were held under guard in the town of Cholm behind the Russian front for fourteen days until they were released—only to arrive in Petrograd to be faced with an order to leave the country by the fastest route and never return. The Russian officials could not understand how two foreigners had ever managed to get so far in the first place.

After months of gathering impressions in Eastern Europe, Reed and Robinson stopped over in Bucha-

*John Reed, Fannie Hurst, and Boardman Robinson in
Washington Square. Reed is wearing a British officer's
field overcoat which he brought back from northern
France.*

rest to complete more articles and drawings before moving on to Serbia, Turkey and, at last, to Italy where they were to board a ship for home. In the baking heat of the Rumanian capital, Reed and Robinson worked in adjacent rooms of the Athenée Palace Hotel, not leaving their worktables until after sundown. Often quick arguments would break out between them, which shed light on Reed's special approach to reportage at the time. Seizing a page of Reed's copy, Robinson would protest that some event Reed had described had not happened precisely that way. Reed would then grab one of Robinson's drawings and, pointing to a peasant woman and a bearded patriarch, exclaim that the woman had not carried such a big bundle and that the man's beard had not been so full. Robinson said that he found nothing exciting in photographic accuracy, that what he had wanted to give was the truthful impression of what he had seen, and Reed answered that this was exactly what he was trying to do.

In the end, both succeeded in their joint aim when Reed's articles, accompanied by Robinson's dramatic drawings, appeared in the *Metropolitan*. What for many people had been merely vague, unfamiliar shapes on the map became transformed into the myriad customs, races, religions, national enmities and national loyalties, of the peoples of the Eastern world. In these articles readers discovered infinitely diversified human fragments

137

A page from Reed's article on Serbia. Illustrated by Boardman Robinson, it appeared in 1915 in the August issue of the Metropolitan.

which nevertheless found a curious unity as they were thrown together in what Reed called "the mad democracy of battle":

It was on the other side of Zastevna, where we stopped beside some ruined houses for a drink, that we saw the Austrian prisoners. They came limping along the road in the hot sun, about thirty of them . . . and among that thirty, five races were represented: Tcheks, Croats, Magyars, Poles, and Austrians. One Croat, two Magyars, three Tcheks could speak absolutely not a word of any language but their own, and, of course, none of the Austrians knew a single word of Bohemian, Croatian, Hungarian, or Polish. Among the Austrians were Tyroleans, Viennese, and a half-Italian from Pola. The Croats hated the Magyars, and the Magyars hated the Austrians—and as for the Tcheks, no one would speak to them. Besides, they were all divided up into sharply defined social grades, each of which snubbed its inferiors. . . .

They had been taken in a night attack along the Pruth, and marched more than twenty miles in two days. . . . A young volunteer of the Polish legion asked eagerly if Rumania was coming in. We replied that it seemed like it, and suddenly he burst out, quivering:

"My God! My God! What can we do? How

long can this awful war last? All we want is peace and quiet and rest! We are beaten—we are honorably beaten. England, France, Russia, Italy, the whole world is against us. We can lay down our arms with honor now! Why should this useless butchery go on?"

And the rest sat there, gloomily listening to him, without a word.

When the articles and drawings were later gathered into a book entitled *The War in Eastern Europe,* Reed noted in the introduction that he and Robinson had missed all the "grand dramatic climaxes." He added that "it was our luck everywhere to arrive during a comparative lull in the hostilities," but he considered this ultimately an advantage for it had enabled him to observe the life of the Eastern nations "under the steady strain of long-drawn-out warfare." These observations only increased his belief in the tragic futility of the European conflict. He returned home in October 1915 more determined than ever to say to his fellow Americans, "This is not our war."

nine:

During Reed's nearly seven months' absence, public opinion in the United States had become even more sharply divided on the war. A great many heavy industries were benefiting directly or indirectly from the sale of munitions to England and France; consequently they leaned toward the side of the Allies and influenced the press to encourage a wave of anti-German sentiment. The sinking of the passenger ship *Lusitania*, by German U-boats, with the loss of over a hundred American lives, had provided fuel for bellicose editorials. Pro-Allied organizations had sprung up, with the National Defense Society condemning the Wilson administration for its "supineness" and the American Rights Committee urging immediate United States participation.

On the other hand, antiwar forces had coalesced and were fighting back. Pacifists had organized the League to Limit Armaments, the American Union against Militarism, and the Woman's Peace Party. The American Socialist Party—unlike European socialists who by and large supported their respective governments after the German parliamentary Socialists voted military credits to the Kaiser— maintained its antiwar position. Radicals found a welcome ally in President Wilson, for he still clung to his policy of neutrality.

Reed was determined to do all he could as a writer to lend his support to the antiwar forces. His faith in the radical movement, in the steadfastness of the President, and in the common sense of the working people, made him confident about his country's political future.

He felt no such confidence, however, about his personal life. Although Mabel had submitted to Steffens's counsel and had made a pretense of love for Reed before his departure for Eastern Europe, any revival of their relationship seemed hopeless now. Mabel had met and fallen in love with the man who would become her next husband—the sculptor, Maurice Sterne. To avoid a painful scene with Reed upon his return, she had induced their mutual friend, the journalist Hutchins Hapgood, to write Reed while he was still in Europe. When Reed had received Hapgood's letter and with it the symbolic ring which Mabel returned, he had thrown the ring into a canal, then written Hovey: "Mabel has broken with me for good, so don't send her any more information or remind her of me."

The familiar sights of New York, however, reminded Reed of Mabel, and it was not long before they met. She was living at Finney Farm in Croton-on-Hudson and in an adjacent house on the same farm lived Maurice Sterne. Mabel suggested that Reed come and live there too, for there was a convenient attic in which he could write. Their relations, of course, would be purely platonic. Reed, whose love for Mabel still lingered, said he would try. His attempt failed utterly, however. He found he could not bear either Mabel's altered affections or the proximity of Sterne. Within three days he had left the farm and Mabel's life for good.

In December he went out to Portland once again to pay a visit to his mother. The same prowar feeling he had encountered in New York prevailed in the conservative circles of Portland society, however, and Reed found the atmosphere unbearable. He had hardly been home a day when he wrote a friend in New York of his longing to be back in Manhattan. His mother was kind, loving, yet absolutely hopeless from a political point of view, and there was not a single person, he added, to whom he felt he could talk.

Two weeks later, however, his mood changed drastically when he came across just such a person—Louise Bryant Trullinger. Mrs. Trullinger was the unhappy wife of a Portland dentist. Like Mabel Dodge, though, she considered herself an emancipated woman and in her heart she was not "Mrs."

John Reed and Louise Bryant

anybody but simply her independent self, Louise Bryant. A freckle-faced girl with red cheeks and beautiful gray eyes, Louise, who was of Anglo-Irish descent, had been born and raised in the West. After graduating from the University of Oregon, she had found a job in a canning factory in Seattle. But she was an aspiring artist and writer, and soon she had begun doing fashion drawings and feature stories for a Portland newspaper—and then she had met and married Dr. Paul Trullinger.

Even before December of 1915, Louise had heard of Reed and admired him, for she was a subscriber to the *Masses*. When she read in the local newspapers of his visit to Portland, she asked Carl Walters, a landscape artist, and his wife, Helen, who were also friends of Reed's, to introduce them. A dinner was arranged, but a few days earlier she and Reed met by chance at an artists' gathering. Reed discovered in the attractive girl a spirit that fairly matched his own, as well as an instant intellectual bond, for she shared his enthusiasm for radical causes. She showed him some of the things she had written, and he liked them. They saw each other often during those few days and slipped into an affair that was far from casual. By the time they arrived at the arranged party, there was no need to ask—the Walterses guessed that Reed and Louise Bryant had fallen in love.

At the end of December he went back to New York where Louise joined him in a few days, after breaking off with Trullinger. In an apartment at 43 Washington Square, near his former rooms in Greenwich Village, they set up housekeeping—or rather nonhousekeeping, for neither one cared much whether a dish was washed or a cupboard set straight. They were too involved in work and in the radical movement. Louise was twenty-eight, the same age as Reed, but he was already a full-fledged writer, while she was ambitious to become one.

He was proud of the lovely and intelligent girl he had rescued from the dullness of Portland and an unsatisfactory marriage. He took her around New York, and he introduced her to his friends. Among them was a young man who drank too much, was shy and morose and introspective but extraordinarily talented, and whom Reed was encouraging to write. Though unknown at the time, one day he would be considered America's foremost playwright—Eugene O'Neill.

Reed liked to have Louise's lively presence beside him now as he worked, on articles and stories, on poems he was selecting for a volume to be entitled *Tamburlaine* which would appear soon, and on political pieces. These last were directed against the growing preparedness movement. There was only a thin line between military preparedness and military involvement, Reed felt, and he used the columns of the *Masses* to say so. In one issue he commented: "The country is rapidly being scared into 'an heroic mood.'" Heroism, Reed felt, lay in another quarter, and in a piece entitled "An Heroic Pacifist" he praised Bertrand Russell who had gone to jail in England for opposing the war. In "At the Throat of the Republic" he exposed the forces behind the preparedness movement. He revealed that the National Security League was dominated by the president of a munitions corporation. He named other industrialists as well—in railroads, in mines, in international finance—who stood to profit from the war. In his zeal he went so far as to mention the millionaire Harry Payne Whitney, a Morgan man and the owner of the magazine which Theodore Roosevelt was helping to turn into an advocate of preparedness, the *Metropolitan*. Reed was jeopardizing his own journalistic future with this kind of writing, but that mattered less to him than carrying an antiwar message to his readers.

He spent the early part of 1916 in New York with Louise, but soon a problem he could no longer refuse to face drove them from the city. The kidney trouble, which had plagued his childhood, had flared up occasionally in recent years but now it suddenly reached such alarming proportions that doctors were considering an operation. First, they decided, Reed needed a rest. In late May he and Louise went to Provincetown where they rented a white clapboard cottage and where their friend O'Neill soon joined them, living in a shack across the street.

There were other friends in Provincetown, too,

147

for each summer the sleepy little fishing town on Cape Cod attracted a group of intellectuals from Greenwich Village. Hutchins Hapgood summered there, and so did George Cram Cook, a professor, and his wife, the novelist Susan Glaspell. It was an ideal spot for Reed. Surrounded by people he knew and liked, he could wholeheartedly plunge into regaining his health without feeling he was out of things. Mike Gold, the left-wing journalist and author of the novel *Jews Without Money*, wrote some years later:

> *I used to see Jack Reed swimming in Provincetown with George Cram Cook, that other socialist and great-hearted adventurer.... I went out a mile with them in a catboat, and they raced through the choppy sea, arm over arm, shouting bawdy taunts at each other, whooping with delight. Then we all went to Jack's house and ate a big jolly supper.*

But Reed, in need of funds with the prospect of hospital costs ahead, had to leave Provincetown in June for Chicago and St. Louis to cover the Republican, Democratic, and Progressive conventions for the *Metropolitan*. He was helped out financially by articles like "The National Circus," which appeared in the September issue with cartoons by Art Young —one of the founders of the *Masses* and a clever political satirist. He rejected assignments that forced him to compromise his principles, however, or to bend his sympathies to fit an editorial opinion with which he didn't agree. Such was the case when the Mexican War became newsworthy again with an American punitive expedition which was led by General Pershing against the rebel Pancho Villa. Reed was approached by John Wheeler of the Wheeler Syndicate, by F. V. Ranck of the *New York American* and by Hovey of the *Metropolitan*, to return to Mexico. But Reed feared that editorial policy in each case would oblige him to glorify the American expeditionary force which, to his mind, was playing an inglorious, repressive role in another country's revolution, and he refused the offers.

Meanwhile, in Provincetown something more than friendship had grown up between Louise Bryant and Eugene O'Neill. She was highly attracted by the moody writer whom she saw every day on the beach, although in the beginning O'Neill, out of loyalty to Reed, had tried to avoid her. All their Provincetown friends knew they were having an affair, but Reed himself seemed not to suspect anything, so skillfully did Louise manage to maneuver between the two men.

Despite the emotional entanglement, O'Neill and Reed retained their friendship which was cemented by their work together with the Provincetown Players. This was an experimental theatre group which staged plays in a shed at the end of a fishing wharf owned by the writer, Mary Heaton Vorse. That summer a short play of Reed's entitled *Free-*

dom figured on one of the bills, while O'Neill's *Bound East for Cardiff*, in which he himself acted along with Reed and George Cram Cook, suddenly revealed a brilliant new talent in the theatre.

All during this time, the need for money forced Reed to keep turning out stories and articles. He did a short dramatic serial for *Collier's* called Dynamite. He wrote "The Last Clinch" and "The Buccaneer's Grandson" for the *Metropolitan*. He covered a strike at the Standard Oil plants in Bayonne, New Jersey, for both the *Metropolitan* and the *Tribune*. He was also negotiating with the editors of the *Metropolitan* about a trip to China where, as the magazine later announced, he would "hold up the mirror to this mysterious and romantic country and we shall see its teeming millions and big forces at work there."

However, all Reed's plans were brusquely interrupted by the necessity of entering a hospital for tests. It was November by now, and he and Louise had returned to New York. They had decided to abandon Greenwich Village for the countryside and had bought a four-room house in Croton-on-Hudson, an artists' colony where the Boardman Robinsons had already settled as well as Max Eastman, the editor of the *Masses*. But though they put a few pieces of furniture in their new home, they postponed the final move until Reed's return from the hospital.

There was always a chance that the removal of

a kidney might prove fatal, and before Reed entered the Johns Hopkins Hospital in Baltimore for examinations which would reveal whether or not surgery would be required, he wanted to marry Louise. She had recently been divorced by Trullinger and had no illusions about the binding nature of legal marital ties. But Reed insisted, and so a few days before he was due to enter the hospital, they went up to Poughkeepsie and exchanged vows in the City Hall. The formalization of her union with Reed meant so little to Louise that she had already started out of the office, when the clerk called her back to give her the marriage certificate.

While Reed spent a week undergoing tests in the hospital in Baltimore, Louise and O'Neill picked up their affair again in New York. She was obviously torn between the two men, but when the doctors decided to proceed with an operation, she went down to Baltimore and stayed with Reed until he was declared out of danger. Then she went back to New York. She and Reed were short of funds, in any case, and they both agreed that it was foolish for her to spend money on a hotel room. But, of course, O'Neill was also in New York.

During his convalescence, Reed received warm and affectionate letters from many of his friends. Copey wrote him from Harvard, telling him that he thought often of him and urging him to send all details about his health. Walter Lippmann came to Baltimore to visit him. Life in the hospital, meanwhile, intrigued Reed, and out of his observations of it came a series of poems entitled "Hospital Notes." But he was not able to forget his money problems and he passed much of his time writing stories to pay his bills.

He and Louise exchanged daily love letters. Her involvement with O'Neill did not seem to lessen in any way her feeling for Reed. She wrote him all the details of moving out of their Village apartment and getting the home in Croton ready for his arrival from the hospital. But she would not go to Croton without him; she would stay in New York until she could go down to Baltimore to fetch him.

Reed was discharged from the hospital in December, and in January of 1917 the *Metropolitan* announced his trip to China. He and Louise, who was to accompany him, began to make their preparations. They went around New York collecting letters of introduction. They were vaccinated and secured passports and passage on a steamship.

A few weeks later, however, the magazine canceled the offer. Pressure on President Wilson from prowar elements had forced him to compromise with his ideal of a "peace without victory" between the belligerents, and in early February he announced the severing of diplomatic relations with Germany. America's entry into the war was obviously imminent, and the editors of the *Metropolitan* felt that a reportage on China was hardly of prime interest. They suggested to Reed that he devote himself to articles related to the "new situation," and they asked if he felt he could come up with something.

It was a rhetorical question, for they knew that Reed, so deeply opposed to the war, could provide no satisfactory answer. In fact, it was merely a diplomatic way of easing him out of the *Metropolitan*. During the past year he had become an increasing embarrassment with his virulent articles in the *Masses* in which he had not even hesitated to attack the *Metropolitan*. They regretted, of course, the loss of a man whom not long before they themselves had labeled the best descriptive writer in the world. As Hovey noted in his reminiscences, the magazine over the years had steered a course which "alternately irritated and placated its advertisers," seasoning socialism with high-quality fiction, setting off Reed with Roosevelt. But maintaining the same careful balance in the present political atmosphere had become impossible. Hovey pointed out:

We could be noble, but not too noble. Could probe the sore spots of society, to take Steffens' figure, but not too deeply where it hurt.... Reed had become what he wished to be, the embodiment of rebellion against the course his country had chosen to follow. The vision that hovered before his eyes—the poet's instinctive dream of a world entirely better—could not be shared ... by a publication widely read and with its feet on the ground of native soil. It was fine for Reed to hate war and say so. But the magazine could no longer be his platform; even if its editors saw with his eyes, which was not the case, it would merely mean the end. The Metropolitan *would have been instantly, cheerfully, squelched.*

The *Metropolitan* had been Reed's chief source of income and now he was forced to look elsewhere. He soon discovered, however, that the numerous high-paying offers from other newspapers and magazines were based, as the *Metropolitan*'s had become, on a tacit promise to conform to editorial attitudes on the war. Reed felt compelled to reject them. Even if he had wanted to, he was incapable of writing anything in which he did not sincerely believe. His habits as a correspondent throughout his career, plus the character of the boy from Oregon, made opportunism impossible. "Reed was a Westerner and words meant what they said," wrote John Dos Passos of him years later. As Reed saw it, he had only one choice—to go on writing what he believed for the starkly dwindling number of papers that were willing to print it.

This choice represented a severe test of character. It meant abandoning the role he enjoyed as a reigning monarch among contemporary journalists and going to work for the *New York Mail* at a reduced salary as a mere feature writer. And in

April of 1917, when America entered the war, it meant abandoning his personal safety as well, for to criticize the government or its policies could bring not only the loss of employment but also a jail sentence of as long as twenty years.

Under the new Espionage Act, which made it a penal offense to refuse to do military service or to obstruct the draft, nearly two thousand people were sent to prison. Another law, the Sedition Act, was directed against people who "used abusive language about the government or institutions of the country." Under it many radicals were rounded up and held incommunicado without benefit of bail and then sentenced to long prison terms. Political meetings were broken up and even innocent bystanders were beaten by the police. Mob hysteria burst out here and there in the country. Vigilantes forced those who took exception to government policy to kneel and kiss the flag. Labor organizers were tarred and feathered. Pacifist preachers were driven from their parishes with whips and clubs.

Reed, however, continued to be an outspoken opponent of the war. A large pacifist rally took place in Washington the night the newspapers announced Wilson's declaration of war with the President's famous words: "The day has come when America is privileged to spend her blood and her might for the principles that gave her birth and happiness." When the news of the President's message swept the hall, Reed mounted to the speaker's platform.

155

"This is not my war," he said, "and I will not support it." A few days later, at the House Judiciary Committee hearings on the espionage bill, at which Reed had requested to testify, he declared, "I am not a peace-at-any-price man, or a thorough pacifist, but I would not serve in this war. You can shoot me if you want and try to draft me to fight—and I know that there are ten thousand other people..."

"I do not think we need to hear from this gentleman any further," interrupted Representative Greene of Vermont.

The chairman, however, ruled that Reed be allowed to continue and he did, backing up his statement with his experiences on five war fronts and upon his observations in Europe which had convinced him that this war was a commercial conflict in which America should take no part.

Though Reed himself did not suffer legal persecution until many months later, he felt other pressures. Old acquaintances, who were afraid to be seen in the company of a radical these days, avoided him. His brother Harry enlisted and wrote him that it was useless to try to buck what couldn't be changed. From his mother in Portland came a letter in which she wrote: "It gives me a shock to have your father's son say that he cares nothing for his country and his flag. I do not want you to fight, heaven knows, for us, but I do not want you to fight against us, by word and pen, and I can't help saying that if you do, now that war is declared, I shall feel deeply ashamed. I think you will find that most of your friends and sympathizers are of foreign birth; very few are real Americans, comparatively."

Reed went on writing, nevertheless—in the *Masses* and, when it was possible, in the *Mail*—against the destruction of constitutional rights by governmental decrees, against the curtailment of labor's hard-won gains, against the greed of war profiteers: "No group or class of Americans should be permitted to have a vested interest in war, nor should they be permitted at the expense of the people to amass enormous sums of money out of the slaughter of mankind."

He went on writing, in fact, until there seemed to be no point in writing any longer, until the war had permeated every phase of American life, and most people had ceased listening. It was then that he began to write for himself, commencing his autobiography with the words:

I am twenty-nine years old and I know that this is the end of a part of my life, the end of youth. Sometimes it seems to me the end of the world's youth, too; certainly the great war has done something to us all. But it is also the beginning of a new phase of life; and the world we live in is so full of swift change and color and meaning that I can hardly keep from

*imagining the splendid and terrible possibilities
of the time to come.*

There was an innate optimism in Reed which nothing could crush, not even a quarrel with Louise which caused her to leave him temporarily. Though her affair with Eugene O'Neill had continued intermittently since their Provincetown days, she succumbed to a fit of jealousy when she discovered that Reed had had a passing affair with another woman. Unable to apply to him the double standard she assumed for herself, she made him feel deeply guilty and contrite. Since her career was in the doldrums, she decided to seize the pretext to go abroad by herself as a war correspondent. Reed was very understanding; he used his influence to get her accredited by the Bell Syndicate, and he found money to pay for her passage to Europe on the *Espagne* in June of 1917. Louise had second thoughts just before sailing; the possibility of losing Reed for good terrified her, and she did not herself understand her own motivations. She sent him a note which said, "Maybe I'll understand better when I get back. I love you so much. It's terrible to love as much as I do."

Reed wrote her that, "In lots of ways we are very different, and we must try to realize that, while loving each other. But of course on this last awful business, you were humanly right and I was wrong. I have always loved you, my darling, ever since I first met you—and I guess I always will."

He was worried about her physical safety overseas, but she was not afraid for herself, as she indicated in a letter to Carl Hovey's wife, Sonya Levien, a writer on the *Metropolitan*'s staff who later became a noted screenwriter in Hollywood: "From the very minute the *Espagne* left New York, things began to happen. We had a little battle with a submarine but... since I discovered that a submarine doesn't frighten me I don't care where I go or what I do—just so I have a front seat."

Her courage was not in doubt, but she never did get "a front seat" in France. Red tape stood in her way, just as it had once stood in Reed's. She couldn't reach the battle lines and not one of the dispatches she sent back from Paris was printed. Her journalistic hopes were quickly dashed, for the moment at least; scarcely a month after her departure, she was already planning to return home. Concerned for her, Reed had been sending money, letters of introduction and ideas for stories, plus assurances of his love. She answered: "I want to come home as much as ever but quite tranquilly, sweetheart, quite whole and healthy—not broken. You said I'd forget things if I was normal. I guess I am, because I've forgotten. Sometimes I wonder how I would feel if it all happened again. I can't think—I can't believe it will.... Sometimes I feel I can't bear it away from my honey."

She decided to sail for home on a French ship in mid-July. Reed would soon have her with him again in New York. The courage this thought inspired in him was reflected in *Almost Thirty:*

> *In my life as in most lives, I guess, love plays a tremendous part. I've had love affairs, passionate happiness, wretched maladjustments; hurt deeply and been deeply hurt. But at last I have found my friend and lover, thrilling and satisfying, closer to me than anyone has ever been. And now I don't care what comes.*

In *Almost Thirty*, too, he revealed the changes which his experiences as a labor reporter had wrought in his political beliefs. When he wrote of the strikes he had covered and how they had confirmed his conviction of the inevitability of the class struggle, he added:

> *I wish with all my heart that the proletariat would rise and take their rights—I don't see how else they will get them. Political relief is so slow to come, and year by year the opportunities of peaceful protest and lawful action are curtailed.*

The political reformer, which that master of political reformers, Lincoln Steffens, had nurtured in Reed, was growing into a revolutionary, and the World War had its place in this process:

> *The war has been a terrible shatterer of faith in economic and political idealism. . . .*

160

There seems to me little to choose between the sides; both are horrible to me. The whole great war is to me just a stoppage of the life and ferment of human evolution. I am waiting, waiting for it all to end, for life to resume so I can find my work.

Reed had placed his trust in Wilson. But the President's policy had collapsed under the pressure of forces more powerful than the presidency which Wilson himself had described in 1913, when he stated, "The masters of the government of the United States are the combined capitalists and manufacturers." And now Reed had faith neither in Wilson nor in the economic and political system under which he had come to believe "that my happiness is built on the misery of other people, that I eat because others go hungry, that I am clothed when other people go almost naked through the frozen cities in winter..." Still, for all this, he greeted the future of his country with hope, when he added: "And yet I cannot give up the idea that out of democracy will be born the new world— richer, braver, freer, more beautiful."

When reports of a revolution in Russia, which had overthrown the Tsar and set up a parliamentary republic, reached America in March of 1917, Reed was not particularly impressed. He felt that medieval Russia, which had never had an industrial—or bourgeois—revolution, had simply caught

161

up with the modern nations of the world and become a capitalist country. During the summer, however, with the emergence of Russian workers', soldiers', and peasants' groups as a dominant force aimed at transforming the capitalist system into a socialist system, Reed changed his mind. Writing in the *Masses*, he said:

We make our apologies to the Russian proletariat for speaking of this as a "bourgeois revolution." It was only the "front" we saw. . . . The real thing was the long-thwarted rise of the Russian masses, as now we see with increasing plainness; and the purpose of it is the establishment of a new human society upon the earth.

If the Russian masses were about to set up a totally new kind of government in a country which extended over one-sixth of the globe, it was obvious that no other contemporary event could compare with it in significance for the rest of mankind. Reed was determined to go to Russia to write about it. Louise was anxious to accompany him and became accredited as a correspondent for a press syndicate. In the conservative atmosphere which now reigned in the country, however, Reed's reputation as a radical, which had been an asset when he had reported on the Mexican revolution and on labor strife in the United States, had become a paralyzing liability. The same newspapers which less than a year before would have been willing to send him anywhere in the world and to pay him the highest salary, were all—though sorely tempted—afraid to hire him. He approached editors in New York, Washington, and Baltimore, but only a few left-wing or avant-garde journals were willing to send him to Russia, and none of these could afford to pay his passage.

It appeared for a while that Reed would miss the greatest reportorial assignment of his career. But Eugen Boissevain, a loyal supporter of the *Masses*, raised the necessary money from a group of sympathizers. The *Masses*, along with the magazine *Seven Arts* and a Socialist newspaper, the *New York Call*, accredited him as a correspondent. The army exempted him from military service because of his kidney operation and the State Department granted him a passport. In mid-August of 1917, he and Louise departed for Russia to witness, he hoped, what he had imagined in his autobiography as "the splendid and terrible possibilities of the time to come."

ten:

The *United States*, a Danish steamer despite its name, carried Louise and Reed past the Newfoundland banks, where it left the usual shipping lanes to sail north and east toward the Arctic Circle. Avoiding waters infested by German U-boats and Allied mines, it docked more than two weeks later in Christiana, now Oslo, in neutral Scandinavia. From there the Reeds moved on to Stockholm and beyond by train, then by ferryboat across the Baltic Sea to Finland. In a Finnish train they journeyed to Vyborg where they changed to still another train for Petrograd, the capital of Russia.

Travel was slow, complicated, and uncomfortable. There were long stopovers everywhere, endless delays and searches at borders, but Reed interviewed people wherever he could. He mingled with crowds of Russian political refugees, persecuted by the deposed Tsar, who were returning to their homeland. He spoke with many of the Socialist delegates—from England, France, Holland, Germany and Russia—who had come to attend an international conference in Stockholm. From these encounters he was able to piece together the story of the events taking place in Russia.

This was not the first revolution to sweep that vast country. Twelve years before—on a Sunday morning in January of 1905—the workingmen of the capital had marched toward the Winter Palace. They had come with their families, chanting hymns and carrying portraits of the Tsar, to present a petition:

> *We, the workingmen of St. Petersburg, our wives, our children and our helpless old parents, have come to Thee, our Sovereign, to seek truth and protection. We are poverty-stricken, we are oppressed, we are burdened with unendurable toil; we suffer humiliation and are not treated like human beings. . . . We have suffered in patience, but we are being driven deeper and deeper into the slough of poverty, lack of rights and ignorance; we are being strangled by despotism and tyranny . . . Our patience is exhausted. The dreaded moment has arrived when we would rather die than bear these intolerable sufferings any longer. . . .*

The Tsar's troops had replied with bullets that killed over a thousand unarmed men, women, and

165

children and wounded thousands more. That Bloody Sunday had aroused bitter resentment in the Russian people. They had begun to listen to a small political group called the Bolsheviks, who were schooled in the teachings of the great German philosopher and economist Karl Marx and guided by a leader considered by both his followers and his foes as a man of extraordinary intelligence and political genius, Vladimir Ilyich Lenin. For some time the Bolsheviks had been trying to convince the Russian masses that the way to achieve freedom was not by begging for it on their knees but by fighting for it in an organized fashion, with a program and tactics that would lead to a new form of society—socialism. As yet untried—except for a few brief weeks in Paris in 1871 when the Communards had held power—socialism, according to the Bolsheviks, was a political system whose time had come.

Under socialism, the Bolsheviks affirmed, workers and peasants would become the owners of the factories in which they now worked and of the land which they now tilled for the profit of others. They, and not a small group of nobles and foreigners, would benefit from the vast natural resources of their country. Instead of a bejeweled monarch whose bored child played with a toy train made of solid gold while the masses in Russia starved, the people themselves would be "tsar."

It was a staggering concept, but Russian imaginations had become inspired by the Bolshevik dream. Strikes had flared up in the big cities, in St. Petersburg, Moscow, Riga, Baku, and barricades had been erected in the streets. But the Tsar had dispatched his troops to destroy the barricades, and the workers had been shot down or jailed.

Peasants had risen in revolt all over Russia, seizing landlords' estates and distributing grain among the hungry. But the Tsarist government had sent its soldiers and Cossacks to quell the revolts, and the peasants had been flogged and tortured.

The Black Sea Fleet had rebelled, with the sailors of the *Potemkin* overpowering their officers and taking command of the battleship. But the sailors had ended up dead or in exile or condemned to penal servitude.

The struggles had continued nevertheless until they had culminated in a countrywide uprising in December. The Revolution of 1905 had openly challenged the power of the Tsar. But the Tsar had answered the challenge, and the Revolution of 1905 had been drowned in blood.

Now, twelve years later, a new revolution had suddenly come into being in Russia. It had broken out in March 1917—just six months before Reed's visit—when the Russian people, weary of the war and facing starvation and unemployment, had taken up arms against the Tsar once again, demanding "peace, bread, and liberty." The Tsar's authority had been weakened by the invading German armies which were decimating his own armies, made up of poorly supplied and poorly led soldiers. He had lost the support of the capitalists, who wanted to be free of the restraints imposed by a regime favoring the great feudal landlords. Harassed from without and opposed by the overwhelming majority of the population within the country, the Tsar had given way and abdicated. In his place the Provisional Government of a parliamentary republic had been set up under a moderate socialist, Alexander Kerensky.

But the political situation was still highly unstable, Reed learned as he approached Petrograd. Tsarist elements were pressing for a return to the old regime, with the troops of General Kornilov's Savage Division massing outside the city. The capitalist class wanted the revolution to go no further, now that they were rid of the Tsar. The workers and peasants, however, were growing discontented with the Kerensky government which had promised them peace and land but had not given either to them. In growing numbers they were joining the Bolsheviks whose program was to continue the revolution by transforming the republic into a socialist society. But not all Socialists agreed with the Bolsheviks. There were many Socialist groups and parties, and they all disagreed violently among themselves as to what should be done. It was a confusing and turbulent period.

Yet when Reed and Louise arrived in Petrograd,

Delegates of the Petrograd revolutionary garrison fraternizing with soldiers of Kornilov's "Savage Division."

they found a jubilant city. General Kornilov, who had sought to impose a military dictatorship, had failed. The Savage Division had not even reached the capital, for committees of workers and soldiers had been sent out to fraternize with Kornilov's men and had convinced them not to fight.

Though its final outcome still remained uncertain, the revolution had momentarily been saved, and the days ahead seemed promising. The mood of the people on the street was infectious. Reed wrote to Boardman Robinson, with whom he had traveled through Russia during their assignment in Eastern Europe two years before:

The old town has changed! Joy where there was gloom, and gloom where there was joy. We are in the middle of things, and believe me it's thrilling. There is so much dramatic to write that I don't know where to begin...

And, indeed, the contrasts were stunning. To find them, Reed had only to walk out the door of the small apartment he and Louise had rented. On the streets the poor stood in long queues from dawn to dusk waiting for a ration of bread that oftentimes was never delivered. Workers and peasants gathered in groups to criticize the government for sabotaging land reforms and arbitrarily jailing revolutionaries. Half-starved soldiers in long, ragged coats harangued crowds and called for mass desertions from the army.

At the same time, as Reed later wrote in *Ten Days That Shook the World*, "ladies of the minor bureaucratic set took tea with each other in the afternoon, carrying each her little gold or silver or jewelled sugar-box and a half a loaf of bread in her muff" to talk hopefully of a German victory or a return of the Tsar or anything that would help solve the difficult servant problem. "Young ladies from the provinces came up to the capital to learn French" and to mingle with the populace in the evenings to hear the world-renowned basso Chaliapin sing or to watch the great ballerina Karsavina dance. One night, between the acts of a performance

Breadlines

171

of a Tolstoy play at the Alexandrinsky Theatre, Reed noticed "a student of the Imperial School of Pages, in his dress uniform, who stood up correctly between the acts and faced the empty Imperial box."

Everywhere, Reed observed, people seemed to be living on their dreams—either of a past they longed to see return or of a future they yearned to achieve. On all sides of him men were talking, arguing, their voices rising in debate. The leaders of the many divergent political parties were all trying to win the masses toward their own particular program. The Russian people, enjoying for the first time in their lives the right of free speech, were answering back, for or against, as they tried to decide which faction to trust.

During his first weeks in Petrograd, Reed went all over the city, talking to everybody he met— merchants, industrialists, influential political leaders, workers in factories, women on breadlines, soldiers from the front. He put his questions in a mixture of English, French, Russian, and German by which he somehow managed to communicate.

From the powerful capitalist Lianozov, known as the "Russian Rockefeller," Reed learned that the revolution was virtually over for "sooner or later the foreign powers must intervene here—as one would intervene to cure a sick child." There was a chance, of course, Lianozov admitted, that such intervention might prove unnecessary for "starvation and defeat may bring the Russian people to their senses." The Bolsheviks did not worry the eminent capitalist, for he added, "The military commander of the district can deal with these gentlemen without legal formalities."

Reed was unable at the time to see Lenin, who was guiding the work of the Bolshevik party from his hiding place in Razliv near the Finnish border. The Kerensky government, less terrified of the pressures on it from the right than those from the left which might sweep it from power, wanted Lenin's life. From Leon Trotsky, however—a major Bolshevik figure whom Reed interviewed in an attic room across a bare table—he learned that the socialist revolution was acquiring momentum. Peasants were already seizing land, and soldiers were gaining increasing control of the factories and of the army. "The Provisional Government is absolutely powerless," Trotsky told Reed. "Only by the concerted action of the popular mass, only by the victory of proletarian dictatorship, can the Revolution be achieved."

From more moderate socialists Reed heard that Kerensky, the head of the Provisional Government, was saving the revolution by inviting representatives of the landlords and industrialists to join his cabinet. Without their support, Kerensky felt, no government could survive. From factory workers and peasants, for whom the words "landlord" and "industrialist" symbolized only another form of the exploitation they had suffered under the tsars, he heard that Kerensky, with his coalition cabinet, was betraying the revolution.

Everywhere Reed went, he heard a different story. But he jotted them all down hastily in his journalistic code of half sentences, a word, a name. At night, in his blacked-out apartment where the city power shortage often limited electricity to a few hours out of the twenty-four, he sat at his worktable. In the flickering light of a taper which Louise had procured from some deserted church altar, he filled out his notes.

Then the next day he would be off again, to a mass meeting—to the press gallery of Kerensky's Council of the Republic—to a session of the municipal assembly. He would stuff his pockets with leaflets people handed out, with proclamations he snatched from the walls of public buildings, with newspapers of every shading he bought at corner kiosks. Daily the piles of literature grew in his room. If the revolution failed, they would turn out to be nothing more than worthless paper, he knew. But if it succeeded, he would have in his possession what no one else was taking the time or the trouble to gather up—priceless and irreplaceable historical documents.

Reed and Louise often went to interviews and meetings together, but as often they separated, for Louise's assignment was to cover the revolution from the woman's angle. While she was interviewing Katherine Breshkovsky, an old revolutionary who now supported Kerensky, or visiting the women of the Death Battalion in Kerensky's army, Reed would attend meetings of shop committees in factories. There he met workers who had taken control of closed-down or inefficiently run factories and had raised wages, lowered production costs, and increased factory output. In Sestroretzk, not far from Petrograd, Reed observed that they had not only organized the transport of food in the town but had built a workers' hospital.

He also visited army units which were fighting the Germans on the northern front and discovered that the soldiers had formed committees which elected delegates to a higher body, called the Iskosol. The Iskosol on its own ordered munitions from Petrograd or oil, wheat, and lumber supplies from Baku and Arkhangelsk, and even at times took command of military actions.

With the Kerensy government unable to suppress speculators and saboteurs or to cope with disorganization in every sphere of life, Reed saw that the common people were gradually taking over the functioning of the country both at the front and in the rear. They were doing so through their councils or "soviets." These small local soviets elected delegates to soviets on a regional level as well, which culminated like a pyramid in the Central Executive Committee of the All-Russian Soviets in Petrograd. Thus a second "government" had come into existence and was operating throughout Russia side by side with the official Kerensky government, but formed by delegates of workers, soldiers, and of peasants on the landed estates.

Reed, as he had written in *Almost Thirty*, had hoped that the "proletariat would rise and take their rights." Now that he was witnessing the process, he made no attempt to hide his enthusiasm. His open partisanship caused no little consternation at the American Embassy in Petrograd, which kept a nervous eye on the small American colony. Bessie Beatty was working as correspondent for the *San Francisco Bulletin*, but there were others who had come to Russia to help the revolutionary forces—Albert Rhys Williams, a clergyman from Ohio; Boris Reinstein, leader of the Socialist Labor Party; and the American radicals, Zorin Gumberg, Bill and Anna Shatoff. Reed's reputation as a writer, however, combined with his revolutionary sympathies, made of him an especially dangerous element in the view of the American diplomats who were not at all sympathetic to the Bolsheviks. They knew that he would not remain silent upon his return to America. After he spoke at a mass meeting in the Cirque Moderne on behalf of Alexander Berkman, an anarchist who was then jailed in America, Ambassador David R. Francis sent secret agents to watch Reed's movements. The agents stole his wallet and discovered letters to the Socialist leaders he had met in Stockholm when he was en route to Russia. He was followed every-where, but as he was an accredited correspondent, the American diplomatic authorities were con-strained to allow him to go his own way for the moment.

As tension mounted between the Kerensky gov-ernment and the soviets, Reed often found himself taking a small tram through the cobblestone streets of Petrograd toward the outskirts of the city to Smolny Institute. Formerly a school for the daugh-ters of the Russian nobility, Smolny was now the nerve center of the socialist revolution. It was the headquarters of the Petrograd Soviet and the Central Executive Committee of the All-Russian Soviet. Countless regional soviets throughout Rus-sia—which ranged in opinion from moderate social-ist to revolutionary Bolshevik—sent their represent-atives to Smolny. Thus Smolny—mirroring the unofficial people's government which spread in a vast network of soviets throughout the country—had become the seat of an unofficial "parliament" in the capital, whose daily increasing influence posed a threat to the existence of the Kerensky regime.

The proportion of this threat became apparent when the Second Congress of Soviets was an-nounced for early November. Soviet delegates from all over Russia would arrive in Petrograd, and if they stood behind the revolutionary Bolsheviks, the Kerensky government would perhaps face a coup d'etat. The threat seemed even more immi-

177

nent when the news came out that the Central Committee of the Bolshevik Party—in a meeting behind closed doors in Smolny which Lenin had attended secretly in disguise—had voted that the time was ripe for the Bolsheviks to seize power, since the majority of the country would support them.

Reed became a familiar figure inside Smolny Institute, where he interviewed party officials and was present at meetings held in the great hall. He later described the atmosphere he found there:

Within were more than a hundred huge rooms, white and bare, on their doors enamelled plaques still informing the passerby that within was "Ladies Classroom Number 4" or "Teachers' Bureau"; but over these hung crudely lettered signs, evidence of the vitality of the new order: "Central Committee of the Petrograd Soviets" ... "Bureau of Foreign Affairs" ... "Factory-Shop Committees" ... and the central offices and caucus-rooms of the political parties. ...

The long, vaulted corridors, lit by rare electric lights, were thronged with hurrying shapes of soldiers and workmen, some bent under the weight of huge bundles of newspapers, proclamations, printed propaganda of all sorts. The sound of their heavy boots made a deep and incessant thunder on the wooden floor. ... Signs were posted up everywhere: "Comrades! For the sake of your health, preserve cleanliness!"

The spacious, low-ceilinged refectory downstairs was still a dining-room. For two rubles I bought a ticket entitling me to dinner, and stood in line with a thousand others, waiting to get to the long serving-tables, where twenty men and women were ladling from immense cauldrons cabbage soup, hunks of meat and piles of kasha, slabs of black bread ...

In the south wing on the second floor was the great hall of meetings, the former ball-room of the Institute. A lofty white room lighted by glazed-white chandeliers holding hundreds of ornate electric bulbs, and divided by two rows of massive columns ... a setting for Grand Duchesses.

Just across the hall outside was the office of the Credentials Committee for the Congress of Soviets. I stood there watching the new delegates come in—burly, bearded soldiers, workmen in black blouses, a few long-haired peasants. The girl in charge—a member of Plekhanov's Yedinstvo group [an almost extinct political faction]—smiled contemptuously. "These are very different people from the first Siezd (Congress)," she remarked. "See how rough and ignorant they look! The Dark People...." It was true; the depths of Russia had been stirred and it was the bottom which came uppermost now.

179

A frightened Kerensky tried to conciliate the "depths of Russia" by renewing his promises of immediate land reforms and a cessation of the war. But at the same time, he ordered those army units which were still loyal to the government to move to the capital to stand ready to forestall an uprising. Then in the early days of November, the government dispatched armored trucks to close down the Bolshevik presses. It ordered Cossacks to patrol the city's streets and commanded the *junkers*, who were students at the officers' school, to train their artillery on the square before the Winter Palace. Kerensky—like the Tsar before him—set out to crush revolutionary Russia.

On the sixth of November, when Reed descended from the tram that took him to Smolny, he noticed that rapid-firing guns had been mounted before the building. Double rows of sentries were guarding the outer gates and an unusually close look was given to the pass he drew from his pocket—a special pass, changed often these days because of the danger of spies, granting right of free entry to Smolny to "John Reed, correspondent of the American Socialist press."

Agitation reigned in the long vaulted corridors on the ground floor. People were running everywhere—distracted couriers, committee members with bulging portfolios, political commissars. On the day before in Smolny, a boy of eighteen, chairman of the Military Revolutionary Committee, had

Red guards at entrance to Smolny

stopped Reed to shake his hand and to announce that the Peter-Paul Fortress—the age-old prison stronghold of the tsars and then of the Provisional Government—had come over to the side of the Soviets. So had a regiment of the army Kerensky had ordered to the capital. All telephones had been cut off by the government, but communication with the factories and barracks had been established by means of the military telephonograph apparatus. The day before as well, one of the dozens of volunteers who waited at Smolny to carry word to the farthest quarters of the city, had informed Reed that everything was ready to move "at the push of a button."

As Reed entered the great meeting hall on November 6, he found it packed. The Petrograd Soviet had been sitting day and night. Many were voicing their support of a *vystuplennie*—a "coming out" of the workers and soldiers—to overthrow the Kerensky government. But, on the dais, one socialist party leader after another was pleading for caution, for calm, for a cooling of revolutionary passions. These leaders were representatives of the moderate socialist parties which had always sought compromise with the Kerensky government. They believed in working for reforms within the framework of the republic. A few months back they had enjoyed the support of the majority of the rank-and-file soviets, but in recent weeks there had been a swing to the left, to the Bolsheviks, and now their speeches were often received with hoots and jeers.

The angry debate continued until midnight and beyond. At four in the morning, Reed left the hall. Whatever was being said on the dais had little relation anymore, he knew, to political realities, for the revolutionary forces had already begun to act. In the outer hall he met a man, with a rifle slung over his shoulder, who told him that a detachment of soldiers and sailors from Smolny had been sent to take over the Telephone Exchange, another the

Telegraph Agency, another the State Bank. . . . The printing shops of the bourgeois press had already been occupied and when Kerensky sent soldiers to attack the printshops, the soldiers refused to obey his orders.

On the steps before the building, Reed caught a glimpse of armed workingmen—the Red Guard. From the distance, he heard the sound of scattered rifle fire. Kerensky's *junkers* were trying to open the drawbridges over the Neva River to prevent factory workers and soldiers of the Viborg workers' quarter from joining the Soviet forces massing in the center of the city. But sailors from nearby Cronstadt, twenty-five thousand strong and confirmed Bolsheviks, were closing the bridges up again.

Still, there was no evidence of real fighting nor was there any the next day—November 7—when Reed arose late, and he and Louise wandered at will over the city.

At the western corner of the Palace lay a big armored car with a red flag flying from it. . . . A barricade had been heaped up . . . boxes, barrels, an old bed-spring, a wagon. A pile of lumber barred the end of the Moika quay. Short logs from a neighboring woodpile were being built up along the front of the building to form breastworks. . . .

"Is there going to be any fighting?" I asked.

"Soon, soon," answered a soldier, nervously. "Go away, comrade, you'll get hurt. They will

come from that direction," pointing toward the Admiralty.

"Who will?"

"That I couldn't tell you, brother," he answered, and spat.

Reed and Louise even managed to enter the Winter Palace itself where they mingled with the *junkers*. These young candidate officers at one moment expressed their longing to be relieved from their frightening posts; the next moment they boasted of their determination to defend the palace to the last drop of their blood. But except for an occasional skirmish, no actual confrontation had occurred by nightfall.

We went into the Hotel France for dinner, and right in the middle of soup the waiter, very pale in the face, came up and insisted that we move to the main dining-room at the back of the house, because they were going to put out the lights in the cafe. "There will be much shooting," he said.... We had tickets to the Ballet at the Marinsky Theatre—all the theatres were open—but it was too exciting out of doors....

He and Louise made their way to Smolny where they discovered an atmosphere strikingly different from that of the night before. Delegates to the Congress had arrived from all over Russia and there was a new militancy in the great packed hall. These

184

*Junkers holding corner of Nevsky Prospekt and Bol-
shaya Morskaya Street*

men and women had brought with them the demand of the soviets on the farms, in factories, at
the front, for the immediate overthrow of the
Kerensky government and the establishment of a
Soviet state. Moderate socialist leaders, who but
twenty-four hours before had been calling for caution and calm, had been demoted by vote and in
their places had been elected a new presidium, the
majority of whom were Bolsheviks.

Even so the moderates were seizing the floor,
their voices rising over the shouts of the crowd, as

185

The Aurora

they pleaded for a peaceful settlement of differences without recourse to arms. "Suddenly a new sound made itself heard," Reed wrote in his description of that night, "deeper than the tumult of the crowd, persistent, disquieting,—the dull shock of guns." The battleship *Aurora*, stationed in the Neva River and under the command of Bolshevik sailors, was bombarding the Winter Palace.

Reed, Louise, and a few of the other Americans in Petrograd, hurried outside. A huge motor truck

186

stood before Smolny. Men were tossing bundles into it. Guns bristled in the back. Reed shouted to them—Where were they going? And the answer came back—Everywhere! The American group showed their passes and climbed aboard.

The great car jerked forward ... past the huge fire by the gate, glowing red on the faces of the workmen with rifles who squatted around it, and went bumping at top speed down the Suvorovsky Prospekt, swaying from side to side. ... One man tore the wrapping from a bundle and began to hurl handfuls of papers in the air.

I picked up a copy of the paper, and under a fleeting street-light read:

To the Citizens of Russia!

The Provisional Government is deposed. The State Power has passed into the hands of the organ of the Petrograd Soviet of Workers' and Soldiers' Deputies ...

The Soviet forces, it was true, had gained control of vital points in the city—the Telephone Exchange, the presses, the railroad stations. Kerensky himself had fled the capital to rally army units against the Soviets. Still, the Winter Palace—symbol of state power in Russia since the days of Peter the Great—remained in government hands, defended by the *junkers*. The truck, heading toward the Palace Square, came to a halt before a cordon

Storming of the Winter Palace

of armed sailors drawn across the avenue. Everyone was obliged to descend. As they managed to slip around the cordon and head on toward the Palace Square, Reed noticed that the guns of the *Aurora* had fallen silent. Silent too were the dark streets in the neighborhood of the Palace. As Reed later wrote:

> *Here it was absolutely dark, and nothing moved but the pickets of soldiers and Red Guards grimly intent. In front of the Kazan Cathedral a three-inch field gun lay in the middle of the street, slewed sideways from the*

*recoil of its last shot over the roofs. Soldiers
were standing in every doorway talking in low
tones. . . . The shooting had ceased.*

*Just as we came to the Morskaya somebody
was shouting: "The junkers have sent word
they want us to go and get them out!" Voices
began to give commands, and in the thick
gloom we made out a dark mass moving forward, silent but for the shuffle of feet and the
clinking of arms. We fell in with the first ranks.*

*Like a black river, filling all the street, with-
out song or cheer we poured through the Red
Arch, where the man just ahead of me said in a
low voice: "Look out, comrades! Don't trust
them. They will fire, surely!" In the open we
began to run stooping low and bunching together, and jammed up suddenly behind the
pedestal of the Alexander Column . . .*

*After a few minutes huddling there, some
hundreds of men, the army seemed reassured
and without any orders suddenly began again
to flow forward. By this time, in the light that
streamed out of all the Winter Palace windows, I could see that the first two or three
hundred men were Red Guards, with only a
few scattered soldiers. Over the barricade of
firewood we clambered, and leaping down inside gave a triumphant shout as we stumbled
on a heap of rifles thrown down by the junkers . . .*

189

Inside the Palace the Red Guards were disarming the frightened *junkers* and, on the promise that they would never take arms against the revolution again, were allowing them to go free. Then someone called out in Russian to make way.

A soldier and a Red Guard appeared in the door, waving the crowd aside, and other guards with fixed bayonets. After them followed single file half a dozen men in civilian dress—the members of the Provisional Government.... They passed in silence; the victorious insurrectionists crowded to see, but there were only a few angry mutterings ...

The cabinet ministers were taken to the Peter-Paul Fortress, and the Provisional Government ceased to exist. In the almost bloodless struggle which had culminated in the storming of the Winter Palace on November 7, the Russian workers had brought into being a new socialist order. Soviet power was now supreme in the land.

During the days and weeks that followed the fall of the Winter Palace, however, these same workers were forced to shed their blood to defend their new society. First Kerensky tried to recapture power militarily, but his armies were defeated and Kerensky fled the country. Then other counter-revolutionary forces were mobilized to sabotage and unseat the new government.

During those troubled and tumultuous days,

Reed stayed on in Petrograd. He observed—he recorded—he expanded his notes to articles—and then he discovered, to his shock, that almost everything he was writing and dispatching back to America was not being printed but was simply being laid away in a drawer. The rising tide of political persecution in the United States had overwhelmed the *Masses;* its offices had been closed down and its editors indicted for sedition. Reed, as well, had been indicted. In August of 1917 he had reprinted verbatim an article from the *Tribune* by a doctor about mental disease in the army and had strung across it the headline: "Knit a Strait-Jacket for Your Soldier Boy." For these seven words he was being called to trial as a traitor to his country.

Reed sent word that he would return to face the indictment, but in the time remaining before his departure, he added to his treasure of notes and experiences. On the day after the historic storming of the Winter Palace, he had been sitting in the great hall in Smolny when:

A thundering wave of cheers announced the entrance of the presidium, with Lenin—great Lenin—among them. A short, stocky figure, with a big head set down in his shoulders, bald and bulging. Little eyes, a snubbish nose, wide, generous mouth, and heavy chin; clean-shaven now, but already beginning to bristle with the well-known beard of his past and future. Dressed in shabby clothes, his trousers much

191

*too long for him. Unimpressive, to be the idol
of a mob, loved and revered as perhaps few
leaders in history have been. A strange popular
leader—a leader purely by virtue of intellect;
colourless, humourless, uncompromising and
detached, without picturesque idiosyncracies—
but with the power of explaining profound
ideas in simple terms, of analysing a concrete
situation. And combined with shrewdness, the
greatest intellectual audacity . . .*

*Now Lenin, gripping the edge of the reading
stand, letting his little winking eyes travel over
the crowd as he stood there waiting, apparently
oblivious to the long-rolling ovation, which
lasted several minutes. When it finished, he
said simply, "We shall now proceed to con-
struct the Socialist order!"*

Reed also had an opportunity to visit Moscow
before he left Russia. Counterrevolutionaries had
been spreading disquieting rumors about the Bolsheviks in order to undermine the first efforts of an
untrained people to run a government. One of these
rumors claimed that the Bolsheviks had destroyed
the palaces and churches of the Kremlin. Reed and
Louise went to investigate. The rumors were un-
true, and Reed made careful notes of the minimal
damage the fighting had inflicted on the beautiful
gold-domed heart of the former capital of old
Russia.

V. I. Lenin

Louise, anxious to return home to write her story of the revolution, left Russia on the twentieth of January. Reed, who wanted to stay until the last possible moment to gather all the material he could, planned to follow in a few weeks. He asked to be

193

made an official courier, as Louise had been, so that he could get his papers through customs without difficulty. Trotsky, now the Commissar of Foreign Affairs, suggested he be appointed Soviet Consul to the United States. Reed accepted, but the news caused a protest in the American press, with the government announcing that it would refuse to recognize the appointment. It seemed it would do more harm than good to the Soviet government as well as to Reed, and it was withdrawn.

Reed left Russia in early February, but when he arrived in Christiana to board the boat for home, he was informed by the American consul that the State Department had refused to grant him a visa. The boat sailed without him and the next one was not scheduled until April, so he was obliged to remain in Scandinavia for two months. Authorities in the State Department apparently believed that during those two months the Soviet government would fall to counterrevolutionary forces; thus whatever Reed would write or say would cease to be newsworthy by the time he reached America.

This view was by no means unusual. In other parts of the world as well as in Russia itself, there were many who hoped and believed that the new social experiment would soon fail. In November Reed had written in a letter to the *Masses:* "The proletarian revolution has no friends except the proletariat."

By now he himself identified wholeheartedly with

that proletariat. He rented a room in Christiana and found work as a stenographer, supplementing his income by doing an occasional article for the Swedish press, and then sat down in his off hours to write the history of the first successful socialist revolution. He had no doubt that not merely in two months but in all the years to come, it would be considered the most "newsworthy" event of the century.

eleven:

While Reed was in Christiana, Louise was working in New York on articles about the Russian revolution. They were published in the *Philadelphia Public Ledger* and other newspapers, and later collected into a book which sold well and enjoyed a brief success—*Six Red Months in Russia*. During Reed's absence, she also wrote to Eugene O'Neill, urging him to see her again. Though Reed was deeply important to her and she was reluctant to jeopardize their relationship, she wanted to renew ties with O'Neill on the old basis. The playwright, who had been in torment after their last separation, was living in Provincetown now with Agnes Boulton, a girl he had recently met and would eventually marry. He wanted to see Louise again and yet was afraid. His feeling for her, and hers for him, died hard. But in the end, though he replied sympathetically to her letters, they did not meet.

Reed returned to New York on the morning of

April 28, 1918. Louise was at the dock to greet him, but she was forced to wait for over eight hours. Federal agents minutely searched Reed's baggage and clothing, and then confiscated his partially completed manuscript plus all the rest of his papers. It was evening before he and Louise could at last go off together to the Hotel Brevoort. Through no fault of his own, Reed had missed the *Masses* trial, which had ended the day before with a hung jury. The judge had dismissed the first half of the indictment but the second still stood; it charged the defendants with obstructing recruiting and enlistment in the armed forces. The government could insist upon holding a new trial if it wished—and it later did. The following morning Reed was obliged to appear in court before a federal judge who fixed his bail at $2,000.

The most serious problem facing Reed, however, was how to recover his notes and papers, for without them he could not write a documented account of the revolution. The government delayed for months. He sent letter after letter to the State Department, but the answers were always the same: when the examination of his papers had been completed, they would be returned to him.

Reed also had to earn a living somehow, and this was not easy because of the intense political repression of radicals. Conscientious objectors were being beaten and set at hard labor. Workers who refused to buy liberty bonds were fired and blacklisted from further employment. The *Masses* had reappeared under a new name, the *Liberator*, and Reed's articles often showed up on its pages as well as in the Socialist *Call*, but the paying magazines were more than ever afraid to touch him. In a letter to Lincoln Steffens in which he asked for help in retrieving his papers from the government, Reed wrote that Oswald Garrison Villard of the *Nation* had told him the magazine would be suppressed if it published him. *Collier's* took a story, set it up in type . . . then returned it. No one else dared to make him any offers.

It was generally acknowledged that Reed was the best reporter in the country. It was generally admitted too that he had the greatest story of the era to tell, and yet he was being prevented from writing it. In fact, during all of 1918 and 1919 Reed published nothing in any nonleft-wing magazine except a short article, "The Case for the Bolsheviki," which appeared in the *Independent*.

There was one avenue left open to him—the lecture platform. Though it paid little, it gave him an opportunity to inform his fellow Americans about the Russian revolution. There was interest in it among working people in the United States. Some Americans agreed with those workers in other parts of the world who saw in it at that time a prelude to world revolution. As the war drew to a close in 1918, workingmen rose against their governments in both Germany and Austria. Italian workers began taking over factories one after the other. A communist regime would soon be installed for a time in Hungary under Bela Kun. Even in Reed's own Portland, Oregon, a Council of Workers, Soldiers and Sailors was organized which recognized the class struggle and sought a Soviet Socialist Republic of the United States. No swift historical transformation seemed impossible, if one considered that Russia had moved from an almost medieval agrarian society to socialism within the space of eight short months. Reed himself was convinced that sooner or later all capitalist countries would become socialist, and through his lectures on the strategy and tactics used by the successful Russian proletariat, he hoped not only to earn a subsistence for himself but to speed this process.

He spoke in Boston, in Newark, and in Brooklyn. When he opened a lecture in Moose Hall in Detroit by addressing the audience as "Tovaritschi..." the assembly, which contained many Russian-born Americans, greeted the Russian word for *comrades* with applause. At that same meeting one hundred and fifty people, chosen at random, were seized by the police and held all night. Reed moved on to New York where he spoke again ... then to Worcester ... then back to New York ... then out to Cleveland.

In Chicago he addressed the Fabian Club and in that city too he saw I.W.W. workers, convicts from the Cook County jail, who had been brought to a federal courtroom for trial. The charge against them was the obstruction of enlistment, but they were as well the objects of a larger campaign against radicalism in general. Reed wrote in an article for the *Liberator* that the prisoners were "one hundred and one *men*—lumber-jacks, harvest-hands, miners, editors... who believe that the wealth of the world belongs to him who creates it." Among them he discovered the familiar face of his old friend from the Paterson strike, Bill Haywood. Many of the defendants were given sentences of five and ten years but Big Bill, who had already been in a cell for nine months, was sentenced along with nine others to twenty years in Leavenworth.

In Philadelphia, Reed arrived to find the hall in which he had been scheduled to speak closed to him, its permit revoked by the city. He drew the audience away to a peaceful side street and began to speak there, when he was arrested for inciting to riot and for seditious statements. His bail was set at $5,000. At Hunt's Point Palace in the Bronx, a few months later, he was arrested again on similar charges, and the bail was another $5,000. By the time Reed appeared for the second *Masses* trial, he was under three indictments with the total bail amounting to $12,000. But the second trial, like the first, ended in a hung jury, and no sooner was it over than Reed returned to writing articles for the left-wing press and to the lecture platform.

Louise had begun to lecture, too. In the early

part of 1919, she left on an extensive tour which included Washington, D.C., Chicago, Detroit, Minneapolis, and San Francisco. An article in *The New York Times* described the impression made by this "demure and pretty girl, with a huge hat, a stylish suit and gray stockings. . . . With the air of an ingenue she hurls darts at government departments, holds people up to ridicule, and with a fearful voice appeals to American fair play to be just to a beneficent Bolshevik Government. . . . In the burst of applause the demure little speaker sits down."

But for all her air of an ingenue, Louise proved that she was able to handle an arduous and taxing schedule. Harder to bear was her separation from Reed, though they exchanged affectionate and frequent letters. She described the warm receptions with which she was met along her way, and he wrote back, full of pride in her accomplishments. Once she asked him for advice on how to address farmers and he outlined his suggestions. More often than not, they wrote of simple things—of their reunion in Croton when she would return, of the garden there, of how much they missed one another.

"How hard it is to be away from you in the spring!" she wrote in late March. "The softness of the air, the fragrance of the flowers makes me dizzy. I toss about restlessly all night . . ." And when she was recovering from a bout of influenza toward the end of her tour, Reed wrote anxiously: "I am aw-

201

fully worried about you. . . . Please hurry home here as quickly as possible. . . . The country is absolutely heavenly. I have been pruning the fruit trees and the grape vine today. . . . All the birds are back, and are going from bird house to bird house asking what the rent is."

In Portland Louise saw Reed's family and though she had been dreading the encounter, it seemed to come off well enough. At one time Mrs. Reed had been sending her son almost daily letters, he wrote Steffens, "threatening to commit suicide if I continue to besmirch the family name." But since then his brother Harry had been demobilized and, despite his fine war record, could not seem to find a decent job anywhere. Harry was trying to sell some real estate Margaret Reed owned, but in the meantime she was short of cash and Reed had had to scrape up some money to send his mother. She was living comfortably enough at the Multnomah Hotel, however, Louise found. Louise lectured at the Public Auditorium in Portland and, as she wrote, "Harry and your mother went and were quite impressed. I seem to stand high with the family at the moment."

After the tour was over, Louise and Reed went to Truro on Cape Cod for two weeks of rest in July, then returned to New York where they rented a small apartment in the Village. They used it as a studio where one or the other could stay when there was an especially pressing deadline to be met or a new lecture series to be prepared.

They depended upon one another a great deal during this period, and pressure from the outside world seemed to make their marriage more secure. Their closeness was especially important to Reed, since so many others who were close to him disapproved of his political activities. He visited Copey on one of his trips to Boston and found his former professor "in a frame of mind that thinks no one is a he-man who hasn't gone into naval aviation." To spare his old friend additional pain, Reed suggested they cease corresponding. Lincoln Steffens wrote Reed, cautioning him pessimistically against trying to fight against the stream, adding that the public mind was "sick" and urging him not to publish political writings for a time. Many of his old college friends were frankly disappointed in him. Art Young recalled in his autobiography:

> *John Reed and Louise Bryant lived at 1 Patchin Place, and I would drop in there of an evening now and then. In memory I can see this dynamic boy, chuckling at some angle of his daily activity and then looking at a pad of paper on his desk as if he ought to be writing instead of chuckling.*
>
> *One evening Louise told me that she had been talking with one of Jack's Harvard classmates. And he said to her: "It's really too bad*

about Jack. He used to write good librettos for light opera. Now I hear he's writing this humanity stuff."

To all appearances, Reed had become a professional revolutionary, yet in fact he was not one. He supported the revolutionary workers in Russia— as once he had supported the striking silkworkers in Paterson and the landless peons in Mexico. He had given up without much regret all youthful dreams of enjoying the best of both worlds. In what radicals called "the class war," he stood with the workers. Still, basically, Reed was a writer. He had made up his mind at the age of nine and he never had wanted and never would want to be anything else.

When the government had at last returned his papers in the late fall of 1918, he had put everything aside and closed himself up for three months of intensive writing. It had taken the State Department more than half a year to decide that it did not really matter anymore if Reed had access to his own files. A civil war was raging across Russia and Bolsheviks were being slaughtered. Fresh victories of the counterrevolutionary White armies over the Red armies appeared to be bringing the defeat of the Soviet government closer every day. Detachments of foreign soldiers from many countries, including the United States, had intervened to give military support to the White generals. To the authorities in the State Department, the end of the socialist revolution seemed at hand.

Reed's collection of documents was extraordinary. There were files of foreign newspapers—the *Russian Daily News*, the *Journal de Russie*, the *Bulletin de la Presse* issued daily by the French Information Bureau in Petrograd. There were proclamations and announcements from the walls of the city dating from mid-September of 1917 to the end of January 1918. There were official publications of all government decrees during the same period as well as secret treaties and documents discovered in the Ministry of Foreign Affairs' files when the Bolsheviks took over. In addition, there were pages upon pages of his own notes.

He discarded the beginning he had written in Christiana and started all over again. Working sixteen, sometimes eighteen hours a day, he approached his subject not only with the passionate sympathy of a partisan supporter but with the cool detachment of a lawyer preparing a brief. From those early days when he had invented stories in a cheap hotel room in Paris, he had come a long way. Years of experience as a professional writer in Mexico, in Europe, in America, were behind him. In recent years he had had to struggle against antagonistic editorial attitudes. All this had developed and heightened his abilities as a journalist until by now—though he had in no way abandoned the colorful style which had become second nature to him—he revealed such a thorough knowledge of his material that no honest critic could assail him. He wrote in his introduction to the book:

> *No matter what one thinks of Bolshevism, it is undeniable that the Russian Revolution is one of the great events of human history, and the rise of the Bolsheviki a phenomenon of world-wide importance. . . . In the struggle my sympathies were not neutral. But in telling the story of those great days I have tried to see events with the eye of a conscientious reporter, interested in setting down the truth.*

The reception accorded *Ten Days That Shook the World*, when it was published by Boni & Liveright in March of 1919, was a tribute to Reed's mastery of journalism. It appeared at a moment when anticommunism in America was reaching a hysterical peak. The federal agents of Attorney-General A. Mitchell Palmer, in the notorious "Palmer raids," were pursuing radicals all over the country, and more than ten thousand people were sentenced to jail. Yet Reed's book cut through political prejudices with its reportorial power and proved fascinating to ordinary readers and critics as well. It received good reviews in the *New York American*, the *New York Sun*, the *Philadelphia Public Ledger*, the *Los Angeles Times*, the *Review of Reviews*. Some papers, of course, were completely hostile; the *Transcript* in Boston demanded to know why a reputable house like Boni & Liveright had sunk so low as to publish such a book. Nevertheless, in the first three months after its appearance nine thousand copies of *Ten Days That Shook the World* were sold, a month later it was in its fourth printing, and even that was no measure of the number of its readers. A single copy often passed through hundreds of hands—in logging camps, in factory towns—until its pages virtually fell away from the binding. The book also made its way to other countries including Russia, where Lenin considered it so faithful a portrayal of the revolution that he wrote a preface which would appear in every successive edition.

After its publication, Reed went back to giving lectures and writing articles for the *Voice of Labor*, the journal of the Communist Labor Party which he had helped to found. This was one of two parties, along with the Communist Party, which had been formed by left-wing elements who had broken away from the Socialists and then had themselves split in turn.

At the same time, Reed was planning future writing projects. Of course he had no idea that *Ten Days That Shook the World* was the last book he would ever publish, for to him it was merely the first installment of a continuing assignment he had embarked upon when he had stepped off the train in Petrograd in the fall of 1917. The assignment would not end until he had completed at least two more volumes whose contents were already taking shape in his mind. He intended to call one of them *From Kornilov to Brest-Litovsk*. It would delve into the function of revolutionary organizations and the structure of the Soviet state. *The Smoke of Insurrection* would follow, containing impressionistic sketches of his first experiences in Russia and those that the future would bring.

To write of these developments, Reed would naturally have to return to Russia and, although at the moment he did not see how to manage it, an unexpected possibility soon arose. In September the Communist Labor Party decided to send him as a delegate to a meeting of the Communist International in Moscow.

The charges against him for inciting to riot and for seditious statements had at last been dropped after the two trials that ended in hung juries. It was impossible for him to leave the country legally, however, for he knew the State Department would never grant him a passport. Through the help of the Irish revolutionary, James Larkin, he obtained forged papers and joined the crew of a Scandinavian boat under an assumed name to work his way across the Atlantic as a stoker. At Bergen he jumped ship—traveled through Finland, hostile to the Bolshevik regime beyond the border, and through Russia itself, still torn by civil war—to arrive in Moscow in December.

He was warmly welcomed by old friends he had

met during the first days of the revolution, and by unnumbered new friends as well whom *Ten Days That Shook the World* had earned him. He was invited to enjoy the privileges of a highly honored guest in a special apartment with special meals, but he refused. In Mexico he had preferred the rough *cuartels* of the common soldiers to comfortable officers' quarters. In Moscow, impressed by the courage of a people who were facing starvation and epidemics they were powerless to check because of a foreign blockade on food and medical supplies, he chose to lodge in a room in a working-class district and to prepare his own meals on a small iron stove.

Lenin, whom Reed saw regularly now, told him he was right to live with the workers—it was the best way to learn Russian and to know Russia—but the Soviet leader chided him for continually overexerting. A man with one kidney ought to take better care of himself, Lenin warned. He had grown fond of talking to Reed, and the two men spent many long evenings in his Kremlin apartment, their chairs hitched up close until their knees touched, often discussing until dawn the trade union situation in America, the civil war in Russia, philosophy, physiology. . . .

It was at Lenin's suggestion that Reed began to write articles for the official publication of the Communist International about the political situation in the United States. Reed conscientiously fulfilled his obligations as delegate of the Communist

Labor Party, but he had returned to Russia for another reason as well. At the first opportunity, he went to visit the countryside and to study the changes that had taken place during his nearly two years' absence. Riding in a sleigh over rutted roads and across ice-covered rivers in the dead of winter, he traveled from city to city, village to village— watching a trial in one, attending a workers' theatre in another, jotting down statistics in still another on the production of wheat and potatoes or on the number of new schools under construction. He spoke to peasants, to soldiers, to workers in factories and, living the sort of life that he loved, he found his notebooks rapidly filling up again. He came back to Moscow charged with new impressions that he meant to set down on paper—only to be confronted with another enforced interruption.

Before his departure from America, both the Communist Party and the Communist Labor Party had been outlawed. Now Reed learned that 123 new indictments had been issued against the members of both organizations. His own name appeared on the list and, as before, he felt obliged to return and face trial, although he was almost certain of being sent to prison. He made two attempts to leave, the first through Latvia, which was unsuccessful, for the Red Army was retreating there and it was impossible to cross the firing lines. The second time he hid in the bunker of a Finnish ship destined for Sweden. But at Abo he was discovered, arrested by the Finnish authorities and placed in solitary confinement.

During the first month of his imprisonment, Reed was not allowed to write or receive letters. In desperation, he thought of a way to publicize his arrest. Through a liberal Finnish woman, Aino Malmberg, he managed to send out a message that he had been put to death. On April 10 New York newspapers carried the announcement of his "execution." Reed's stratagem worked: the State Department was forced to announce that he was still alive in Finland. He and Louise were at last able to communicate and he wrote to her, "I am informed by the Finns that I am kept in prison at the request of the United States government." Louise was frantic and did everything in her power to secure Reed's release. Soon Reed learned that a significant number of people back home had rushed to his assistance, including an uncle of his, General Burr, and his old editors from the *Metropolitan*, Hovey and Whigham, who, if they did not approve of Reed's ideas, were appalled at the methods taken to stop him from expressing them. At the same time the Russians were negotiating with the Finnish government. In exchange for Reed's release they offered two counterrevolutionary Finnish professors whom they had arrested. The Finns accepted the proposal and, early in June, Reed was set free. The American consul refused him a passport, however. He had no choice but to abandon his intention of returning home and to go back instead to Moscow.

Reed was impressed with the changes that had taken place in the city during his three months' imprisonment. It was spring and the great gardens were bright with flowers. Destroyed walls had been repaired. Public buildings had been repainted. Chaliapin was singing *Faust* to packed theatres. Most of Russia, in fact, was charged with optimism despite the terrible devastation and the harsh living conditions, for the tide had turned in favor of the Soviets and the civil war was at last approaching an end.

His Russian friends, however, were not at all happy to observe the changes that had come over Reed. His long weeks of confinement in a dank cell in Finland, where he had been forced to subsist on a diet of raw fish, had left him gaunt and weak. It was obvious to all who knew him that he was no longer a well man. But he plunged into activity again, attending meetings of the second Congress of the Communist International, writing reports, making speeches. As a special delegate to a Congress of Oriental Nations in Baku, he journeyed in an armored train through the southern Ukraine— still in the throes of civil war—and beyond it to the shores of the Caspian Sea. There he spoke to two thousand Asian delegates—Persians, Armenians, Hindus, Chinese. On the way back to Moscow, the train was attacked by bandits. Reed begged the Red Army squad which was starting out in pursuit

Reed among the delegates at the Congress of Oriental Nations in Baku a few weeks before his death.

of the marauders to allow him to accompany them, and he went along in the battered peasant wagon on which they had mounted their machine guns.

Upon his return to Moscow, he found Louise who had just arrived from the United States to join him. She had brought with her a letter from his mother in answer to one he had written from prison in Abo. Margaret Reed had reconciled herself to accepting her son as he was, and the letter had some of the flavor of C.J.'s independent view of life:

213

What you say about feeling selfish makes me feel badly, dear. Don't ever feel like that. You are doing what you think is right—that is all any of us can do in this world—and if we don't do it, we're all wrong. Except for fear for your personal safety, the rest is all right in my eyes if you feel that it is.

Louise was alarmed by Reed's thinness and pallor. Brushing aside her concern for his health, he took her about the city to visit Lenin and Trotsky, to attend *Prince Igor*, to tour the art galleries. At the same time he continued to attend meetings and to write reports.

Less than a fortnight later, he came down with what was apparently influenza. He went on writing through his illness but after another week, when the doctors discovered that it was not influenza but typhus, he was taken to the Marinsky Hospital to be put under the care of the leading specialists in Moscow. Even in his hospital room Reed asked that the stenographic record of his talks at the Congress be brought to him so that he could make revisions. But by that time he no longer had the strength to lift a pencil . . . and he never would again, for the spotted typhus had already begun to run its deadly course and the medicines that might have saved his life lay unobtainable somewhere beyond the blockaded ports of the country.

John Reed died on October 17, 1920, a few days

before his thirty-third birthday. For a week his body lay in state in a silver coffin at the Labor Temple guarded by soldiers of the Red Army. On the following Sunday, thousands joined in the funeral procession in Red Square where he was buried beneath the Kremlin walls. On November 14, Louise Bryant sent Sonya Levien Hovey of the *Metropolitan* a letter destined for Max Eastman, editor of the *Liberator*. In it Louise described her last days with Reed:

We had only one week together before he went to bed. And we were terribly happy to find each other.... His clothes were just rags. He was so impressed with the suffering around him that he would take nothing for himself. I felt shocked and almost unable to reach the pinnacle of fervor he had attained ...

Of the illness I can scarcely write—there was so much pain. I only want you all to know how he fought for his life. He would have died days before but for the fight he made. The old peasant nurses used to slip out to the chapel and pray for him and burn a candle for his life. Even they were touched and they see men die in agony every hour ...

On the day of the funeral we gathered in the great hall where he lay.... It was cold and the sky dark, snow fell as we began to march. I was conscious of how people cried and of how the

215

banners floated, and the wailing heart-breaking
Revolutionary funeral hymn, played by a mili-
tary band, went on forever and ever.

I do not remember the speeches. I remember
more the broken notes of the speakers' voices.
I was aware that after a long time they ceased
and the banners began to dip back and forth
in salute. I heard the first shovel of earth go
rolling down and then something snapped in
my brain. . . . After an eternity I woke up in my
own bed.

But I have been in the Red Square since
then—since that day all those people came to
bury in all honor our dear Jack Reed. I have
been there in the busy afternoon when all
Russia hurries by, horses and sleighs and bells
and peasants carrying bundles, soldiers singing
on their way to the front. Once some of the
soldiers came over to the grave. They took off
their hats and spoke very reverently: "What
a good fellow he was!" said one. "He came all
the way across the world for us. He was one of
ours . . ."

Louise lived for another sixteen years. In 1923,
in Paris, she married William Bullitt, a former
Washington correspondent and later a member of
the State Department and the first American Ambassador to the Soviet Union. Louise and Bullitt
had a daughter, but the marriage was unhappy and
ended in divorce seven years later with Bullitt re-

taining custody of the child. Louise returned to New York where she lived in the same Village apartment she had once shared with Reed at 1 Patchin Place. But the past could not be recaptured so easily. She fled back to Europe again where she died in Paris, of a cerebral hemorrhage, in 1936. She never truly recovered from her loss, as Art Young revealed in his autobiography:

> *Poor Louise committed slow suicide—went the sad road of narcotic escape. Only a few weeks before she died she sent me a postcard from her Paris studio at 50 rue Vavin.*
>
> *"I suppose in the end life gets all of us," she wrote. "It nearly has got me now—getting myself and my friends out of jail—living under curious conditions—but never minding much. . . . Know always I send my love to you across the stars. If you get there before I do—or later—tell Jack Reed I love him.*

Louise's loss had been painfully personal, but there were also countless numbers of people all over the world who had never known Reed but who had admired and respected him. When the news of his death had first reached America, thousands of jailed radical workers had received it in tragic silence. The press in the United States, which had been quick to revile him during his lifetime, had written respectfully of him and his work. Copey, who had always cursed the Bolsheviks, had been deeply bereaved. He had spoken to the students of English 12 of Reed's loyalty and courage ... that courage which had caused Reed to believe, even during his last painful hours, that something, somehow, would rescue him from oblivion.

Reed was right, in a way. Something has. Hundreds of articles, two eloquent books—and a masterpiece, *Ten Days That Shook the World*. It stands alone as an unsurpassed record of living history.

The world is still being shaken by the political repercussions of the social upheavals which John Reed set down as an eyewitness in 1917. For well over half a century people have been arguing bitterly over the concepts of socialism, capitalism, evolution, revolution.... A few have argued over Reed himself—former radicals like the anarchist Emma Goldman, Benjamin Gitlow, and others, who in later years became opposed to the Soviet regime. They have tried to enlist Reed as an ally, claiming that he suffered a last minute disillusionment with socialism when he is said to have murmured to Louise, "Caught in a trap ..." But this phrase can be interpreted in many ways; at best it is hearsay evidence, for nothing that Louise herself wrote bears it out. In any event, arguments over Reed's meaning are not only vain but beside the point—the problems they raise are not his but belong to those who live after him. When John Reed clubs were formed by American radicals after his death, Margaret Reed sent a letter to Steffens protesting that

Foreign editions of Reed's classic Ten Days That Shook the World

her son might not have approved the use of his name. Steffens, who understood Reed perhaps better than anyone else, answered that the last time he had seen him, Reed had berated him for not coming out straightforwardly for world revolution. Steffens added:

And, Mrs. Reed, I'm afraid you are wrong about his not standing for the use of his name by the clubs. My impression is that Jack would approve or, if he objected, he would have complained only that the John Reed Clubs do not go far enough. He might say to them what he said to me that night on a street corner in New York: "Go on—the limit!"

In the thirty-three years of his life, the boy from Oregon indeed followed the advice he gave Steffens. He went the limit.

Books by John Reed

Insurgent Mexico (D. Appleton & Company) (International Publishers)

The War in Eastern Europe (Scribner's)

Ten Days That Shook the World (Modern Library) (International Publishers)

Daughter of the Revolution and other stories (Vanguard Press)

Tamburlaine and Other Verses (Hillacre)

The Day in Bohemia or, Life among the Artists (Hillacre)

Sangar (Hillacre)

Articles and short stories which appeared in the *American Magazine*, *Collier's*, *The Masses*, the *Liberator*, and *The Metropolitan* can be found in certain libraries.

Books by Louise Bryant

Six Red Months in Russia (George H. Doran Co.)

221

Photocredits

Culver Pictures, Inc: frontispiece
Harvard College Library: 16, 18, 19, 22, 26, 28, 98, 99, 144, 213
The Huntington Library, San Marino, California: 72
Ivan Kobozev: 188
L. Leonidov: 193
Pirie MacDonald: 45, 49
Novosti: 171, 181, 185, 186
Count Jean de Strelecki: 136
Tass: 169
Paul Thompson: 115
Underwood & Underwood: 94

Index

Almost Thirty (Reed), 7, 19–20, 28, 43–44, 47, 93, 109, 116, 157, 160, 176
American Federation of Labor, 61
American Magazine, 47, 50, 75
American Rights Committee, 141
American Union against Militarism, 141–142
Anderson, Sherwood, 59
Andrews, Robert, 47–48
antiwar attitude, Reed's, 131, 132, 140, 142, 146–147, 153, 155–156, 157
Aurora, the, 186, 188

Baker, George Pierce, 21
Beatty, Bessie, 176
Behrman, S. N., 21
Bellows, George, 59, 133
Bennett, Arnold, 77
Berkman, Alexander, 176
Berlin, 124
Beveridge, Albert J., 124
Bloody Sunday in Russia, 165–166
Boissevain, Eugene, 163
Bolsheviks, 166, 167, 168, 173, 176–178, 180, 182, 183, 185, 186, 192, 204, 205, 206, 208, 217
Bostonian, the (cattleboat), 31–35
Boulton, Agnes, 196
breadlines in Russia, 171
Breshkovsky, Katherine, 175
Bryan, William Jennings, 117
Bryant, Louise, 143, *144,* 145–147, 149, 150–152, 158, 162, 163, 164, 168, 170, 174, 183–184, 186, 192–194, 196, 197, 200–203, 211, 213, 214, 215, 216, 217, 218
Bullitt, William, 216

Call, New York, 163, 198
Carranza, Venustiano, 91, 102, 108
Cather, Willa, 42
Cedar Hill, 1, 3, 5, 7, 10, 12, 17
Century, 50
civil war, Mexican, x, 90–111
Cobb, Irvin S., 51
Coleman, Glenn, 57
Collier's, 51, 198
"Colorado War, The" (Reed), *115,* 116
Communist Labor Party, 207,

223

208, 209–210
Communist Party, 207, 210
Cook, George Cram, 148, 150
Copeland, Charles Townsend
("Copey"), 25–26, 27, 29,
47, 50, 51, 80, 88, 112, 151,
203, 217
Cosmopolitan Club, 21, 22
Crane, Stephen, 42

Davidson, Jo, 73
Davis, Richard Harding, 121,
129
Day in Bohemia (Reed), 133
Diana's Debut, 24
Dodge, Mabel, 61, 63, 70–72,
73, 74, 83, 84–88, 113, 116,
117, 123, 134–135, 142, 143
Dos Passos, John, 154
Dramatic Club, 21
Dreiser, Theodore, 42
Dunn, Robert, 121, 124, 125,
129
Dunne, Finley Peter, 90
Dutch Treat Club, 51, 55

Eastern Europe, war in, 130,
134, 135
Eastman, Max, 56, 59, 150,
215
Eliot, T. S., 29
Espionage Act, 155
*Everymagazine, an Immoral-
ity Play* (Reed), 55

Ferber, Edna, 77
Filon, Madeleine, 40–41, 43,
84
Filon, Marguerite, 40
Flagg, James Montgomery, 51
Foote, Arthur, 51
Francis, David R., 176
Freedom (Reed), 149–150

"German Trenches, In the,"
125–127, 128
Giovannitti, Arturo, 59

*Girl of the Golden Tooth-
brush, The* (Reed), 23
Gitlow, Benjamin, 218
Glaspell, Susan, 148
Globe, New York, 47, 75
Gold, Mike, 148
Goldman, Emma, 218
Gorky, Maxim, 59
Great War, the, 4. *See also*
World War, First
Green, Charlotte, 1–3, 4, 5, 39
Green, Henry, 2, 3
Greenwich Village, New York,
16, 42, 47, 52, 57
Guereca, Longinos, 106
Gumberg, Zorin, 176

Hagedorn, Hermann, 15
Hapgood, Hutchins, 61, 75,
142, 148
Hapgood, Neith, 61
Harvard College, 13–30, 46,
51, 56
Hasty Pudding Club, 24, 37
Haywood, Bill, 60–62, 67, 105,
200
Hill, Joe, 75
Hovey, Carl, 77–79, 80, 90,
100, 112, 113, 116, 117, 122,
124, 127, 128, 142, 149, 153,
159
Hovey, Sonya Levien, 215
Howard, Sidney, 21
Huerta, General Victoriano,
91, 116
Hughes, Rupert, 51, 77
Hurst, Fannie, 77, *136*

Independent, the, 198
Insurgent Mexico (Reed), x,
27, 112
International Workers of the
World (I.W.W.), 60–61, 82,
83, 199
Intimate Memories (Dodge),
84

James, William, 20
John Reed Clubs, 218, 220
Jones, Robert Edmond, 48, 74, 82, 83–84
junkers, the, 180, 183, 184, *185*, 187, 189, 190
Jusserand, Ambassador, 130

Kemp, Harry, 59, 81
Kerensky, Alexander, 168, 173–175, 180, 181, 183, 187, 190
Kerensky government, 168, 173, 175, 176, 177, 182, 185
Kornilov, General, 168, 169

Lampoon, Harvard, 15, *16*, 24, 31, 48
Larkin, James, 208
La Tropa, 104, 107, 108
League to Limit Armaments, 141
lectures, Reed's, 198–200, 207
Lenin, Vladimir Ilyich, 166, 173, 178, 191–192, *193*, 209, 214
Levien, Sonya, 159, 215
Lianozov, 172
Liberator, the, 198, 200, 215
Lindsay, Vachel, 59, 81
Lippmann, Walter, *19*, 23, 48, *49*, 73, 110, 130–133, 151
London Daily News, 36
Lowell, Amy, 73
Ludlow, Colorado, mini strike, 113–116
Lusitania, the, 141

Mail, New York, 154, 157
Malmberg, Aino, 211
Marin, John, 73
Masses, The, 56, *57*, *58*, 59, 60, 70, 81, 89, 118, 119, 135, 145, 146, 148, 150, 153, 157, 162, 163, 191, 194, 197, 198, 200
Mercado, General, 92–93

Metropolitan, the, 76–78, 81, 89, 90, 97, 100, 110, 111, 112, 113, 115, 116, 117, 118, 120, 122, 125, 128, 129, 130, 133, 135, 137, *138*, 147, 148, 149, 150, 152, 153, 154, 211, 215
Mexican notebooks, pages from Reed's, *98–99*
Mexican war, x, 90–111, 116, 149
mineworkers, Ludlow, Colorado, *115*
Modestino, 62, 74, 82
Monroe, Harriet, 55
Monthly, Harvard, 15, 17, *18*, *19*, 24, 48
Morristown School, New Jersey, 9–12, 14
Moscow, 192, 212, 213, 214
Movers and Shakers (Dodge), 84, 85, 87

National Defense Society, 141
National Security League, 147
New Republic, the, 130, 131
New York, 43–51, 52, 54–63, 87, 130–134, 143, 145, 147, 150, 196, 202

O'Neill, Eugene, 21, 146, 147, 149, 150, 151, 152, 158, 196
Oriental Nations, Congress of, 212, *213*
Orozco, Pascual, 93, 95
Osgood, Alan, 16, 47, 48

pacificists, 141, 155
pageant in Madison Square Garden, 62–63, 70, 73–76, 81–83, 84, 86
Palmer, A. Mitchell, 206
Paris, 37–38, 39–40, 84, 85, 120–122, 123
Paterson, New Jersey, strike in, 61–70, 75, 76, 77, 81, 83, 86, 89

Peirce, Waldo, 31, 33, 34–35, 36–37, 40, 85
Pershing, General, 149
Peter-Paul Fortress, 190
Petrograd, 168–172, 175, 176, 191
Petrograd revolutionary garrison, *169*
Philadelphia Public Ledger, 196
poems by Reed, 51, 53–54, 55, 86–87, 152
politics, 46, 52, 131, 134
Portland, Oregon, 1, 8, 12, 42, 51–52, 117, 143, 145, 146
Portland Academy, 7–8, 9, 14
Potemkin, 167
Price, Lucien, 15
Provincetown, 116, 147–149

Ranck, F. V., 149
Red Guards, 183, 188, 189, 190
Red Square, Moscow, 215, 216
Reed, Charles Jerome (C.J.), 3–4, 6, 12, 28, 30, 39, 42–43, 46, 51–52, 118, 213
Reed, Harry, 3, 7, 24, 42, 156, 202
Reed, John, *28, 136, 144*
Reed, Margaret, 4, 5, 113, 117, 143, 156, 202, 213, 218
Reinhardt, Max, 84
Reinstein, Boris, 176
Revolution of 1905, Russia, 165–167
Reyes, Julian, 106
Robinson, Boardman, 135, *136,* 137, 138, 140, 150, 169
Robinson, Edwin Arlington, 55, 73
Rockefeller, John D., Jr., 115
Rogers, Robert, 47, 48
Roosevelt, Theodore, 3, 118, 129, 130, 147
Rubenstein, Arthur, 86
Russell, Bertrand, 59, 147
Russian Revolution (1905), 165–167
Russian Revolution (1917), x, 161–165, 167–194

Sandburg, Carl, 59, 81
Sanger, Margaret, 73, 74
Saturday Evening Post, 32, 50
Savage Division, Kornilov's, 168, *169*
Sedition Act, 155
Seeger, Alan, 48
Seven Arts, 163
Shame of the Cities, The (Steffens), 46
Shatoff, Anna, 176
Shatoff, Bill, 176
Shay, Frank, 47
Six Red Months in Russia (Bryant), 196
Sloan, John, 59
Smart Set, 50
Smolny Institute, 177–179, 180–*181,* 182, 184, 187, 191
socialism, 166
Socialist Club, 23, 46
Socialist Party, American, 142
Socialists, 46, 168, 185, 207
Soviets, 177, 181, 187
Steffens, Lincoln, 28, 44, *45,* 46–48, 52, 55, 58, 60, 73, 90, 134, 160, 203, 218, 219, 220
Sterne, Maurice, 142, 143
stories by Reed, 32, 50, 56, 59
"Storm Boy," x, 52
Street, Julian, 50
strikes, x, 62–70, 75, 81, 83, 86, 89, 113–116, 160, 167. *See also* pageant in Madison Square Garden
Sunday, Billy, 138–134

Tamburlaine (Reed), 146
Tarkington, Booth, 129
Ten Days That Shook the World (Reed), x, 170, 206–207, 209, 218, *219*
Tit for Tat (Reed), 23

Trend, 51
Tresca, Carlo, 67
Trotsky, Leon, 173, 194, 214
Trullinger, Louise Bryant, 143.
   See also Bryant, Louise
Trullinger, Dr. Paul, 145, 146,
   151

"University Club," 33
Urbina, General, 103, 104

Villa, Pancho, 91–92, *94*, 95–
   97, 100–102, 109, 149
Villard, Oswald Garrison, 198
Voice of Labor, 207
Vorse, Mary Heaton, 149

Walters, Carl, 145
Walters, Helen, 145
War in Eastern Europe, The
   (Reed), 140
Wells, H. G., 77

Western Club, 23, 24
Wheeler, John, 149
Wheelock, John Hall, 15
Whigham, H. J., 90, 122
Whitney, Harry Payne, 147
Williams, Albert Rhys, 176
Wilson, Woodrow, 115, 116,
   117, 118, 119, 141, 142, 152,
   155, 161
Winter Palace, Petrograd, 165,
   184, 186, 187, *188*, 189–190,
   191
Woman's Peace Party, 142
World, New York, 92, 110, 112
World War, First, 117–128,
   152, 155–161, 198. *See also*
   Eastern Europe, war in

Young, Art, 59, 148, 203, 217

Zapata, Emiliano, 91